DANIEL CHAK

The Product Manager's Guide

Strategy, Psychology and Leadership at Work

Contents

Introduction

No one really knows how the game is played
  The art of the trade
  How the sausage gets made
  We just assume that it happens
  But no one else is in
  The room where it happens.

No one really knows how the
  Parties get to yes
  The pieces that are sacrificed in
  Ev'ry game of chess
  We just assume that it happens
  But no one else is in
  The room where it happens.

I wanna be
  In the room where it happens.
  Oh, I've got to be in
  The room where it happens.

– Aaron Burr, Hamilton the Musical

Why Product Management

I can't count the number of times people have told me, "You have my dream job!" The product manager job is highly coveted. I'm grateful to have been a Product Manager at Google for more than eight years, where I gained the experience that I put into this book.

Why do so many people – even those who already have great jobs in other roles at Google – want to become product managers? What is so special about this job?

The product manager is at the center of the work that goes into creating the tech products millions of people rely on and enjoy using every single day. They're responsible for the strategy, for the trade-offs that are considered and the decisions that are ultimately made. As such, they are *always* in the room where it happens, and as the lyrics from Hamilton say, that's where a lot of people want to be.

Product management is, in my humble opinion, the most exciting role in any company. It's also a role with a lot of responsibility. In exchange for being in the room and owning decisions, the product manager is also responsible for the outcomes and the consequences. Sometimes the outcomes are good and sometimes they are not so good.

For some people, having this responsibility and the potential for failure can be a heavy burden. But for those who are energized by risk, who are comfortable not knowing all the answers ahead of time, and who are skilled in driving clarity where there has only been ambiguity, a career in Product Management can be just what the doctor ordered.

Why this book, why now, why you

> *"If you hire an engineer and they're no good, you can have them work on something small and it doesn't matter. If you hire a PM and they're no good, the whole team is screwed."*
> *—My former manager, who will remain anonymous*

Most books available on Product Management today focus on landing the job, not on doing the job. Those books are necessary because a Product Management job is very difficult to land. In many tech companies, there's typically only one product manager for every ten to fifteen engineers, so there's room and necessity for companies to be extremely selective.

The Product Management interview process at top tech companies is notoriously challenging. Candidates are expected to pass interviews touching on product design, product strategy, market dynamics, and analytical thinking. Many companies, including Google, require product managers to pass a technical interview equivalent to one given to a new CS grad. Doing well in the interviews isn't just about having the right answers. Product management candidates are also expected to structure their interview responses with the same level of sophistication as business strategy consultants. (Consequently, some of the best prep you can do for Product Management interviews is the same case interview prep prescribed for landing a consulting role at McKinsey, Bain, or BCG.)

But learning about product management doesn't end at getting hired. That's only the beginning!

The Product Management discipline continues to be an opaque topic. It's learned on-the-job by going through a series of product launches that require the product manager to work with people across the company. Those people are all looking to the product manager for direction, while the product managers are often just learning how to do the job themselves.

Confounding the learning process is that the product life cycle can be long, with each stage requiring different types of attention and care from the product manager and the team. Until you've been through a few launches as a product manager, it can be difficult to even know who you should be reaching out to inside your company, and when, to move things forward. It can take a number of product launches before you start to see the *patterns* in what you've done, and have built a network of people to get the job done. For first-time product managers, it can literally take years to fully understand their jobs. This is not a joke!

Product managers who I've recruited to work at Google were graduates of top undergrad and MBA programs, have had PhDs, and came from top consulting companies. Despite their impressive credentials, they still needed to learn how to do the challenging, on-your-toes job of Product Management that I'll explain to you in this book.

This book strives to help Product Managers see the structure in their job so they can be successful sooner. When you know what's coming next, you can be thoughtful about how you approach the job and be deliberate rather than reactive. When you know all the people in your company who have a role to play in the full product life cycle, you can get the product out the door smoothly. This book introduces Product Managers to the key people they'll work with so they can leverage the expertise of others immediately rather than spin their wheels trying to do everything themselves. And it introduces Product Managers to all phases of the product life cycle so they can anticipate what's coming next in their jobs.

It's a good thing you're reading this book because the world needs more excellent product managers. Product managers are the essential catalyzing agents in large organizations who enable teams to deliver great products. As a product manager, you can have a huge impact on the company you work for by helping your team achieve results faster than they thought possible and with greater impact. And by focusing your team's efforts toward achieving transformational goals, you'll have a huge impact on the world.

How do you become a Product Manager?

Unlike many jobs for which college coursework directly prepares you, there were no Product Management courses available when I was in college, and there was certainly no Product Management major. Seeing this gap, Google created a rigorous two-year Associate Product Manager (APM) program to train graduates fresh out of top universities to be product managers on the job. This highly selective program is still thriving at Google today. Unfortunately, it's harder to get into than Harvard.

Luckily, there are ways to become a product manager besides the APM program at Google. Business schools teach many of the skills you need, and most actually do have Product Management courses these days. Many MBA grads become PMs directly out of their business school programs, and most big companies like Google and Amazon recruit directly from these programs.

Many PMs have a background in strategy consulting. With its rigorous attention to frameworks and methodical deconstruction of problems, strategy consulting is great preparation for being a PM. Not only are these techniques especially useful in responding to interview questions – they also translate into an instinct to focus on the big picture and take the long view.

Many product managers in tech companies come from technical backgrounds, have computer science degrees, or were practicing software developers for some time before becoming product managers. Having such a background is not a strict requirement for being a good product manager, but it helps to have a working understanding of how software works, and have a good intuition for what's easy and what's hard. That threshold level of understanding is key to be able to discuss engineering decisions and trade-offs directly with the engineering team.

Entrepreneurship teaches you product management, too. Many people say that a PM is "the CEO of…" whatever product they're managing. But being a PM is not just for the CEOs. In small startups, early employees "wear many hats". As the company grows, jobs get more specialized. If you're one of these early employees who like having their hands in all aspects of what the startup is doing, then taking on a PM role as the company grows is the way to go.

If you have your sights on a big company like Google but going to business school, landing a strategy consulting job, or being a startup founder doesn't fit your near-term life path, working as a PM at a smaller company is another great way to develop PM skills. Often smaller companies are more likely to take a chance on someone eager to step into a PM role for the first time than big companies whose recruiting departments look for candidates who fit a pre-existing mold.

Taking on PM responsibilities in your current company is a great path, too. Building on the domain expertise you have from your current role, try taking on some product management responsibilities. Within Google, so many people are eager to switch from their current job role into the product management job role – whether from engineering, business development, marketing, or program management – that Google runs an internal curriculum called "Path to PM", with numerous courses on all aspects of being a product manager to support employees in making the transition.

Ultimately, you've got to just go for it. If you're not a product manager already, by reading this book, you're taking your first step.

Who this book is for

If you're interested in becoming a product manager, are a new product manager, or simply want to get another perspective, then this book is for you.

For new product managers starting their first role, this book is your cheat-sheet for how to do your job from Day One. This book contains a timeline for product development and all the templates you'll need to do the job.

For those interested in the career of Product Management, this book will teach you what being a Product Manager is all about. I'll guide you through the basics of product management – both from a technical and team perspective.

For veteran product managers, this book will put into words what you've been doing all these years. Having a language around the practice of Product Management will give you the means to focus on aspects of your work and hone your skills.

The skills that make you a good product manager at work can also help you achieve your goals in life. So you don't actually have to *be* a product manager to get value out of this book. You can also use this book to pick up the tools of our trade and apply them to your day-to-day life.

What's in this book

First, we'll go through *Orientation*. In Chapter 1, I'll break down the job description of a PM. What a product manager can expect to do varies over the course of a product manager's career. I'll explain what the job looks like at different career stages.

Next, I'll introduce you to the team. The product manager can't get anything done in the organization without the partnership of others. A PM orchestrates the work of others, helping a broad team of people build and deliver a successful product to market. You'll need to know who all those people are in order to seek them out and bring them into your product process.

In Chapter 2, I'll explain *vision* and *insight*. Product management isn't an administrative job. Great product managers are visionary and insightful leaders who deeply understand users and how they respond to products. The product manager is expected to provide direction to the team. Many people wonder where this direction comes from. I'll show you some techniques you can use to spark your own creative process and train your vision and insight muscles over time.

In Chapter 3, I'll take you through a framework for the full *product life cycle*. The end-to-end product journey, from ideation to launch can be long. This framework will help you achieve your product goals by breaking down the journey into distinct phases of *Align*, *Define*, *Plan*, *Execute*, *Launch* and *Land*. Each of these steps has its own work, deliverables and challenges that you'll need to master as a product manager.

In Chapter 4, I'll discuss *Validation.* show you techniques for validating the product throughout the product development life cycle. Decisions should be made based on data, not opinions, so having methods to ensure you're on the right track throughout a lengthy product development process is essential to ensure you don't waste the team's effort and your time on a product that is unlikely to find traction.

In Chapter 5, I'll walk you through *Tools of the Trade.* These *artifacts* are documents that you'll need in the course of your work to solidify understanding and communicate with others. A PM generates lots of documents to keep the team on track, the ones I'll discuss are absolutely required items for your toolbelt:

- A *two-pager* and *vision deck,* each of which explains a new product or feature at a high level to get the point across quickly to stakeholders.
- A *product requirements document,* or PRD, to get specific about the actual product outcomes you seek.
- A *project plan to* lay out the work items that need to be completed to turn the specification into a reality.
- A *roadmap* to lay out how you'll achieve your goals in concrete increments.

In Chapter 6, I'll discuss *Process.* A product manager brings order to the chaos. Having some structure around the year, quarter, and day-to-day can help the team stay on track.

Finally, in Chapter 7, I'll talk about *Influence*. I'll describe specific soft skills that will help you be successful as a leader. To be effective, you'll also need to develop the craft of selling your idea, of bringing people together, and of carrying the team through rough patches. I'll give you tips to build strategic working relationships and craft your narrative. And I'll help you focus in order to achieve great results, and scale to accomplish more than you can do on your own.

Let's get started.

1

The team

In this chapter, we'll get to know the entire team that the Product Manager works with to build and launch the product. The product manager's fingerprints are everywhere. They are a master coordinator, but all the real work is the work of others. Without the team, there is no product, no launch, no victory.

It's critical that the product manager understands who all the players are and how to make use of their talents to put together the best product possible. Beyond knowing who the players are, good product managers have some working knowledge in as many functional areas as possible, too. For example, be ready to sketch out product flows and propose appropriate language for the product. Be ready to consult on the technical design and help the engineering team weigh the pros and cons of multiple approaches. Be prepared to do data analysis on your own.

But remember that the product manager's main job is to paint a picture of the future for the team and then put together the framework that will facilitate the team's building of that future. Through guiding and empowering others, the product manager delivers tangible, valuable outcomes for the company. The product manager does not actually do the work of all these team members.

This section is somewhat skewed toward a technology product company. Your organization may have additional roles that I don't mention here, like scientists in biotech. It doesn't mean the role isn't significant, only that you'll have to figure out on your own how that function fits in and how best to leverage it.

The Core team

The core team in technology products is made up of a lead from Product, Engineering, and User Experience (UX). In the early stages of a project, when the direction and the broad strokes are being determined, the PM is likely to pair with only the engineering and UX leads, who will help refine the product vision. I call this the Product-Engineering-UX triad. The triad's task is the definition, design and development of the product.

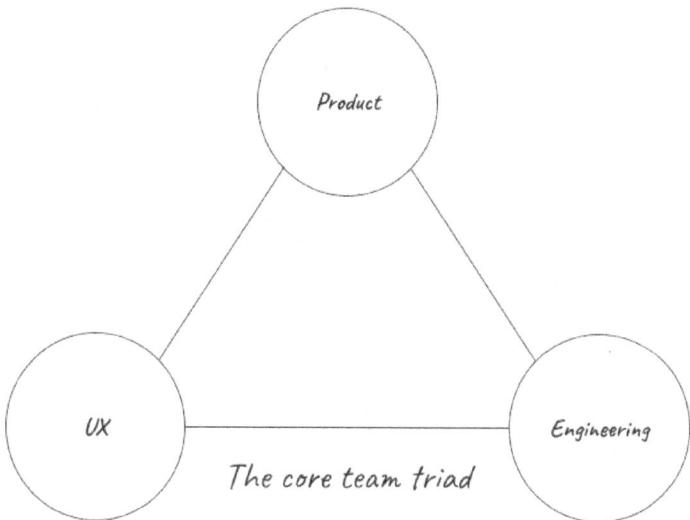

Product

UX

Engineering

The core team triad

This triad must gel for things to go well. A gelled team has synergy and it can feel like each function can read the others' minds. That happens best when the engineering lead has a good product sense, and the product manager and the UX lead have some sense of the limits of technology.

The product lead brings to the table the product and user goals. The UX lead will help give the product tangible shape in the hands of a user, steering the product in a direction that will make sense to customers. At this stage, a great engineering lead will push the PM and UX leads to think as big as possible, highlighting possibilities rather than focusing on limitations.

But ultimately, the engineering lead will help to keep the vision within reach of technical feasibility. Once the product direction is better understood, and the project has the green light, individual contributors on the engineering and UX teams will join the work.

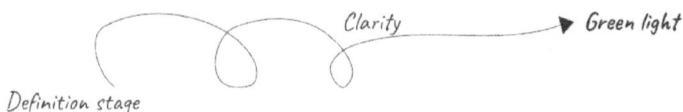

Clarity — Green light

Definition stage

Engineering

In a tech company, without engineers, there's no product. The engineers build the actual product that ships to customers.

Engineers fulfill a critical role throughout the process. In the early stages of a product, engineers consult on the requirements. Engineers know best what is possible and easy, possible but hard, risky, or downright impossible.

After the product requirements are established, engineers author technical designs that specify how the product will be implemented. Typically this is done by a team lead or an architect. The design should satisfy the product requirements as well as the engineering teams' own requirements regarding technology stacks, security, scalability, architecture best practices, etc.

With a technical design agreed upon, the eng team implements the product. Once the product is tested and meets the criteria, the team productionizes it, meaning they ensure the product will work under the heavy loads and harsh conditions of the real world, where failures are not only possible but probable. During productionisation, the team ensures system redundancy, instrumentation for logging, monitoring, alerting, etc.

With all systems ready, the engineering team makes the product available to the public – the product "launches." From here on out, the team maintains the product, fixing bugs as they are discovered, and releasing updates to patch issues. During this maintenance mode, the team is likely to be simultaneously consulting on designing the next set of features with the Product and UX team.

Product managers should be comfortable reviewing an engineering team's technical design. This is a key check on whether the engineering design will fulfill the product requirements or not. The PM should be able to judge if the design will paint the team into any corners that will make it harder to extend the product down the line.

User Experience (UX)

There is a maxim in product development that "the user experience *is* the product." This couldn't be more true. Even if a product is technically capable of getting a job done, if the user can't figure out how it works, or if it's very cumbersome to use and the user prefers *not* to use it, the product is next to useless.

The measure of how easy it is to accomplish goals using a product is called its *usability*. The UX team are the experts in designing the steps the user undergoes to accomplish their goals with the product. The easier it is to find and accomplish the main tasks and the more intuitive the flows, the higher the product's usability.

A larger UX team will have specialized roles. I'll talk about the responsibilities of each of those roles and how it fits into the entire team below.

User Experience Designers

UX designers are the magicians of the product experience. Their role is to ensure the product is usable. Some key considerations of UX designers are below:

Information architecture. Information architecture, or *IA*, refers to how information and actions are organized in an application. Is it easy for the user to find entry points to the tasks they want to complete?

It's easy to spot products that were lacking a UX designer. For example, when the interface looks like it's directly exposing the database tables, you can safely bet the UI was designed by the engineer who designed the database schema. Another dead giveaway is when you see a long list of actions with no clear organization. In this case, you might imagine a business owner presented a list of "musts" to an engineering team to develop, but without any context as to when and why the actions are relevant to the user.

Good UX recasts the capabilities of the system into a presentation that makes it easy for users to accomplish their most critical tasks, while maintaining the ability to do everything else.

Good UX is based on how users expect to accomplish a task, not on how it most easily maps to the underlying data representation in the storage system.

Design patterns. Is the experience consistent? For example, when editing text, will the text be edited inline, or will the product pop up modals where the user makes edits? Can the user pick and choose what information they edit, or will the experience be designed around wizards that enforce a sequence to how information is collected from the user? When there's feedback for the user, does it always appear in the same place, and in the same format so the user knows where to look for it? Lack of consistency poses a direct challenge to usability.

Wireframes, mocks, and redlines. User Experience Designers create the actual designs for the product experience that the engineering team will build.

The key tasks a user should be able to complete are called "user journeys", and the UX team helps define them and bring them to life visually. I'll cover User Journey definition in detail when I discuss the Product Requirements Document later in this book.

There are three levels of detail for conveying the UX, each at different levels of fidelity, and useful at different stages during the product development:

Wireframes show the elements of the screen in extremely low-fidelity blocks that indicate where screen elements like menus, images, and buttons go. They're useful for quickly assembling a series of screens and showing how those screens fit together, often with arrows connecting showing how navigation elements link the screens together. *When the user clicks this navigation element, they'll be taken to this screen.* Wireframes are useful for deciding what the right "flows" are from one screen to the next, and whether the right elements are on each screen. They are too low of fidelity to discuss the visual design itself.

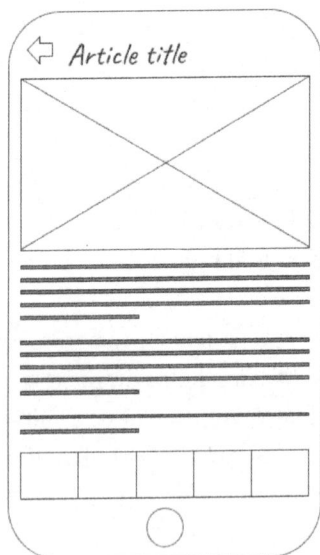

A product wireframe

Mock-ups, or just *mocks,* show the same screens as a wireframe, but at a higher level of fidelity that matches what a user would actually see when using the product. If you were to take a screenshot of an actual application, the screenshot matches the level of fidelity expected of a mock. Once the user journey flows are decided on via wireframes, mocks help the team see what the product will actually look like. In mocks, the actual colors, imagery, and design elements are shown as they'll be shown in the final product. The product text, or "copy", is also shown as it would appear in the final product.

Mocks themselves can be at higher or lower levels of accuracy – *rough mocks* on the first pass may have incorrect spacing between elements, or placeholder text. *Final mocks* are produced once the design has settled down and should match a screenshot of the final developed product.

Redlines are the design spec that the UX team hands off to engineers. They're an overlay on top of mocks that show the exact sizing and spacing of elements. Much like an architectural spec, this treatment of the final mocks enables the engineering team to build a pixel-perfect product. Redlines detail exact font sizes, spacing, image sizing, margins, etc.

User Experience Researchers (UXR)

User Experience Researchers, or UXR for short, can help with user *needs* research before you get too deep into design work through user surveys.

User Experience Researchers are instrumental help validate

that a product design is usable through ability studies. This is typically done by bringing in real users to provide feedback on the product.

The product doesn't have to be working in order to get user feedback. Often the mocks created by the UX team are sufficient to walk study participants through hypothetical situations.

With static mocks, the researcher can ask the study participant to describe what they see. They can talk the user through what the user would do in hypothetical scenarios and what they would expect to happen based on their actions. The user researcher can manually swap in new mocks to progress the user journey.

A static set of mocks is often called a "paper prototype," as in the good old days it was made with printouts laid out on a table in front of the study participant. There are now many tools that allow a static prototype to be turned into a clickable prototype (Figma or InVision are popular choices). The UX designer can wire up the mocks by defining clickable regions that take the user to another mock. A clickable prototype can give the user a real feel for the product without a single line of code having been written by the engineering team. This is a valuable tool for understanding if users "get it" before a lot of investment has been made.

I'll go through these types of validation in more detail in Chapter 4, *Validation*.

Visual Designers, Production Designers

Recall the continuum from wireframes to mocks to redlines. A UX Designer spends most of their time in the earlier phases of wireframes and rough mocks. The UX designer spends their time thinking about the user goals and the holistic experience of using the product. The visual designer spends their time in the later phases in the final mocks and redlines phases.

Imagine a scenario where the team has agreed upon wireframes and flows that represent 100 product screens. In addition, a handful of key screens have been turned into rough mocks that the team and stakeholders have approved. In order for the engineering team to build the product to pixel-perfection, they still require redlines for all 100 product screens, which represents a lot of work to be done. When a visual designer's main job is to apply a well-understood visual language to a large set of wireframes or rough mocks and generate final mocks suitable for redlines, they may be referred to as a *Product Designer*.

In summary:

- A *User Experience Designer* spends their best time thinking about user goals and holistic product experience. They lay out the critical user journeys that show how a user accomplishes their goal with the product. They may define reusable *experience design patterns* that can be seen again and again in different circumstances.
- A *Visual Designer* spends their best time thinking about how screens look one at a time. Their focus is on

11

making the product look great. They're expected to have creativity around the product's visual design and may define reusable *visual design patterns* that can be repurposed in different circumstances.

- A *Production Designer* spends their best time taking visual designs and user experience flows and turning them into final mocks and redlines that can be used by engineers to build a pixel perfect product. A production designer needs to have mastery of the tools, but isn't required to have the creativity that a visual designer might.

In a small team, UX designers may fulfill all three of these roles. As the team grows, specializing can occur. Production design can be time consuming and doesn't require the same high-level skills as UX design does.

Interaction Designers

Interaction designers are less common. They focus on designing interactions and visual feedback. For example, transitions between screens, or gestures on touch screens or trackpads and how the product responds to those gestures. Some well-known examples are pulling a browser window down to refresh the page, or pulling down in an email program to check for new messages. The iPhone's swipe-to-unlock feature is another example of interaction design.

Many interactions are parts of operating system or toolkit design libraries, and the same ones get reused over and over again. That's good for consistency. Users know what to expect and products behave in similar ways. For this reason, it's not always necessary to have an interaction designer on the team. If the product has a large surface area justifying frequent interaction consultation, or if the product itself is heavily interaction-oriented, then a specialized interaction designer may be needed.

User Experience Writers

UX Writers write the text, or *copy*, that appears in the product.

UX writers will develop a voice for the product, which can be codified into a style guide. Is the writing terse and neutral or upbeat and cheerful? Is it designed for a specific reading level? Are contractions allowed? Will it be in Standard English or British English?

The style guide may also define acceptable word choice so the language throughout the product is consistent. For example, does the rental app refer to the thing being rented as a *car* or an *automobile*?

While the UX writer is the expert on the writing style, what they write has to be accurate. Often a PM will provide the information that needs to be conveyed, and the PM will need to review the proposed copy to ensure no critical information was lost.

Final copy is typically also reviewed by Legal and Policy teams to be sure claims are accurate and don't expose the company to risk.

> *Recommended reading for Product Design*
>
> *A foundational book that can help you build your product design thinking is The Design of Everyday Things, by Don Norman. First published in 1988, this is a timeless classic that covers the gamut of product design from teapots to lightswitches. This book may seem dated, but even as the state of the art changes from desktops to mobile phones to wearables, the fundamentals of human-centered product design have stayed the same.*

The Cross-functional team

While the cross functional team isn't tasked with the product definition or development, they fulfill critical roles in ensuring the success of the product's development and launch.

Project / Program managers

This role goes by lots of names, depending on the company: project manager, program manager, technical project manager, and potentially others. In this book I'll just say "project manager" to encompass all flavors.

Project managers do all of the coordination at the technical level. They build an understanding of how long the product development process will take, and they keep the engineering team on track toward launch.

Working with the engineering team, the Project Manager creates a project plan that enumerates all the tasks required to complete the project, with time estimates for each. They regularly meet with the engineering team to update the plan and project out new completion dates.

Once the product is in a testable state, project managers can assist in, or even own, the triage of incoming bugs. They may provide a first pass at prioritization of bugs for the engineering team, and lead weekly bug review meetings.

Throughout this process, the project manager should have some mechanism of keeping the broader team informed of project progress – for example, a weekly update email. The update should enumerate the major workstreams and the status of each; any metrics available, such as open and closed bug counts; and risks the team is working through.

In a smaller team that doesn't have a dedicated project manager, the Product Manager should be ready to step into this role. Even when there is a project manager to support the project, the Product Manager should work extremely closely with them to ensure the product is on track, and that prioritization of feature and bug work is correct.

The Product Manager is ultimately responsible for the product delivery, and so should be involved in any decisions that delay the product launch or change the scope.

Data science

Today's applications collect troves of data about how users use the product, and in many cases, information about the users themselves. Data scientists can help make sense of the mountains of data, finding trends in usage patterns, or figuring out which users are having success and which are having trouble with the product. Whereas the UX researchers gathered qualitative data about how users *anticipated* they might use a product, data scientists can provide concrete data about how users *actually* are using your product.

Data scientists can also help design experiments to test different approaches to how the product is presented to the user or how it behaves. Using statistical methods, they can design the experiment methodology, including how many users must be in each experiment group and how much data needs to be gathered for the result to be statistically significant.

> *Recommended reading for Data Science*
>
> *My all-time favorite book about data is The Visual Display of Quantitative Information, by Edward Tufte. This book won't give you the technical skills to become a data scientist, but it will give you a better sense of how complex quantitative information can be expressed in an understandable manner. Just as product managers need to think about the usability of the product's user interface, it's also valuable to think about the usability of data.*

Marketing

Often people say "marketing" when they mean "advertising." But marketing is a critical function involving much more than simply buying ads.

Marketing involves understanding who the customers are, how many of them are out there, and where to find them. The entire population is likely not your audience – but who is? Further, it involves understanding their needs: what is important to them, what features are appealing, and how valuable is each feature? Marketing also involves understanding customers' motivations for buying and how they go through the buying process.

A marketer should also understand the competitive landscape of alternative options that customers have. Who are the other players, what products do they offer, and how are those products differentiated? Who are the target customers for those products? Beyond obvious competitors, what alternatives do users have? For example, pizza restaurants don't only compete with other pizza restaurants; they compete with all types of eating out, as well as with eating in. Understanding all of these facets of the market as well as the trends is *market research*.

A strong sense of the market gleaned through thorough market research and experience will help shape how your product is presented to the market. The core product you're building may not change – e.g., all airlines are selling airplane seats and get you from point A to B – but how you position your product almost certainly should change. Market positioning has many

17

knock-on effects in terms of pricing, features, and support. There's a world of difference between a flight on Southwest targeted at economy flyers traveling between smaller cities and a business flight in United's Polaris class.

A final component of marketing is the messaging and the operational component of advertising.

In collaboration with the product team, the marketing team puts together the Go To Market plan. This plan details the target customers, where and how the product will be announced and how it will be advertised.

Recommended reading for Marketing

Crossing the Chasm, by Geoffrey Moore, is an absolute must-read. This book defines the phases of a product's adoption life cycle and who is the customer in each phase: Innovators, Early Adopters, Early Majority, Late Majority, and Laggards.

For each life cycle segment, Moore explains what motivates customers to buy a product. Because different segments are motivated in different ways, it's incumbent on the product manager, working with the marketing team, to understand who is the company's current target, and how best to win them over.

Blue Ocean Strategy, by W. Chan Kim, Renee

Mauborgne, et al., is an invaluable book about market positioning. If your product is largely a commoditized good, this book presents six paths of exploration that can lead to adapting your product to reach a totally new audience.

Product operations

Many products have operational elements, meaning ongoing work that must be done once the product is launched.

This can be anything from content moderation to inventory management, and depends entirely on what your product is. As a Product Manager, you'll need to work with the product operations team to ensure there's a plan in place for all aspects of your product's post-launch operation, as well as the right amount of staff to keep the operations active.

Customer support

Customer support is a critical function to ensure users can get help when the product is falling short of providing the value that was promised to users.

Sometimes the actual product delivered doesn't meet the customer's expectations, and in these cases there need to be ways for the customer to return the product for a refund.

Sometimes the product's usability falls short, and customer

support can help users realize the value that they've paid for by guiding them through some rough parts of the UI.

And sometimes the product has actual flaws that may not have been caught during the product development process. In these cases, customer support can be an invaluable part of the team. As the front-line that hears directly from customers who are experiencing problems, the customer support team should be properly deputized to gather information from users, and report user complaints to the product team for further investigation.

Finance

The finance team monitors the financial health of the business. They can be a tremendous help in the product development process by building models to validate whether the product lineup, pricing, and sales expectations are going to meet the business's financial objectives. Given the proposed product offering and price points, for the proposed target segment, will it be profitable, if so, when?

Consulting functions

I've split out legal and policy from the cross-functional team. They're typically more of a safety check on your plans rather than a generative part of the product development process. Bearing that in mind can help to modulate how you, as a Product Manager, make use of their advice.

Legal

Startups sometimes see gray areas of the law as business opportunities. Uber, Airbnb and cryptocurrency companies like Coinbase are excellent examples. The taxi industry is highly regulated, but Uber launched its ride hailing service around the world without any explicit government approval. The incumbent taxi drivers revolted, and many cities temporarily banned Uber until regulations could be established.

Similarly, Airbnb started its home sharing service without much regard for local renting regulations. Many municipalities eventually limited who could operate an Airbnb and at what volume, and extracted heavy taxes from Airbnb operators. But those regulations and taxes came years later, once Airbnb was already a success.

Cryptocurrencies, which bear remarkable similarities to securities, are only beginning to be regulated by the Securities & Exchange Commision as of this writing. During these gaps of regulation, companies who arrive willing to take risks can reap massive rewards.

In risk tolerant companies that move aggressively into uncharted territories, the legal teams are part of the assault, working reactively to clear the way for the company to continue operations under murky legal frameworks.

More established companies tend to be less tolerant of risk. In larger companies, the role of the legal team is not to reactively clear the way, but to proactively steer the team away from risks.

In a risk-averse company, certainty is preferable to uncertainty, and new business opportunities in underregulated domains are viewed with a high degree of suspicion. These legal teams are likely to provide the product team with a dour viewpoint on anything the product team might want to do.

Of course, you can't break the law, and where there is clear law the product must stay within it. But where the law is unspoken or murky, the Product Manager needs to understand the *risk* and determine whether the risk is acceptable. Thus, not everything the legal team points out is necessarily a veto. Understanding the risk tolerance of your company is key.

Policy

Where the law does not offer an opinion, often a company will form its own policies on a matter to regulate the company's behavior.

A policy team will help the Product Manager ensure their product adheres to the company's existing internal policies. A transgression of a company's policies typically is a veto on the product. However, if the policies can be shown to no longer meet the needs or expectations of the customers, regulators, and the market, the policies may be changed to accommodate the new product and market realities. Often, it's a product manager who must forge the way to make such changes to clear the way for innovation.

Some product offerings may require that new policies be developed in order for the team to be comfortable with the launch. For example, before launching a product that collects and publishes user generated content, policies for what kind of content is acceptable should be developed. By developing policies in advance, the team will know how to respond when questionable content is found. An internal policy team can help the Product Manager define appropriate policies for their product launch. Policy teams often have a legal background, or will consult with legal teams as needed.

Now that you've met the team, get ready to work with them.

2

Vision & Strategy

If you don't know where you want to go, then it doesn't matter which path you take.
  —The Cheshire Cat; Lewis Carroll, Alice in Wonderland

The product manager is tasked with the roadmap for their product. But how do you know what you should be doing in the future, let alone in the present? It's easy to pick projects to do next based on their adjacency to your current projects. Or to iterate on the current work the next iteration is well understood: just take a few features off the backlog and build in the same way tomorrow as you built yesterday. These options, while safe and easy, are not always the right thing to do. Of course they work for a while, but at some point, they stop working, because the market is in need of a step change rather than an incremental iteration.

In this section, I'll talk about the related concepts of strategy, vision and insight. Establishing a vision keeps all the team's projects on a single focused track toward a desired future outcome.

I'll start by discussing what a *lack* of vision and strategy can feel like, so that you can spot it.

Then I'll talk about what vision and insight are and how you can start to build your muscles in this area. Having vision and insight starts to cross over into *innovation*, so we'll get a taste of innovation in this book, with pointers to where you can learn more.

Knowing where you're going

Random walk

In 1827, the botanist Robert Brown described a phenomenon, now called Brownian motion, based on his observations of the pollen of the plant Clarkia pulchella immersed in water. The pollen seemed to move about completely at random.

"Random walk" is an algorithm that models Brownian motion. You start with a point on a line, a plane, or in 3-dimensional space. At each time step, you randomly assign a new direction for the point to move in. Below is a computer generated image showing a random walk in two dimensions after 25,000 steps. The moving point gets somewhere, but it also gets nowhere in particular. At the time when the motion starts, you have no idea where the point will end up. Certainly, it did not take the shortest path to get there.

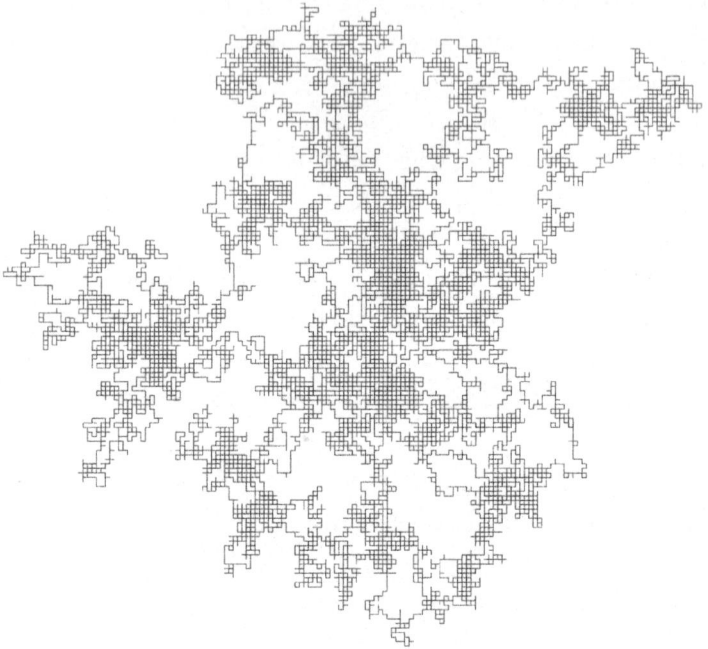

A random walk of 25,000 steps

When we have no vision, we do something that we know *can be done*, without much risk, rather than what we know *must be done*, even if we have no idea yet how to do it. When we have no vision driving our next actions, then we're not doing much better than a random walk.

Imagine a day where you wake up without a plan. You sit down and respond to the emails that have found their way into your inbox. When it's time for lunch, you open the fridge and eat whatever is in there. When you take a break, you open an app on your phone. You scroll and scroll down an infinite wall of images and shocking headlines. You go down this rabbit hole, then that rabbit hole, until you realize you've been scrolling and clicking for 30 minutes and you don't even remember where you started. You go back to email. When you're done for the day, you watch Youtube. As soon as one video is done, another starts immediately. Finally the day is over. How exhausting all that was. Good thing it's time for bed.

An interesting property of Brownian motion was discovered years later by Albert Einstein. The motion of the pollen is actually not determined by the pollen itself – it's influenced by the random motion of the water molecules beneath the pollen. At first glance you can imagine the pollen has some agency, choosing to go this way and then that on the surface of the water. In fact, the pollen was just along for the ride, its motions dictated by the capriciousness of the water molecules. The endless stream of emails, the infinite content in scrolling apps, and the videos that play one after another – they are the water upon which we float our boat. As much as we think we're in control, we're actually pulled by the undercurrents of what's around us. When we random walk, we are the pollen, getting taken along for a ride atop these endless streams of distractions.

This style of living or working can be described as "looking busy", but it is not particularly productive, and it doesn't get you anywhere in particular. You can random walk over the course of a day, and you can random walk over the course of a lifetime.

Planning at work can succumb to the random walk phenomenon. When we have no vision for where we want to go, this quarter's goals are often an iteration on last quarter's goals. Or we pull from a backlog of old acceptable ideas, rather than motivate ourselves toward bold new ones. Or we look to our customers to set our roadmaps for us – scratching their itches but not really making a dent in the universe.

Hill climbing

Hill climbing is a real human condition reduced to mathematical terms.

Imagine a curve that has many peaks and valleys. Now pick a point on that curve at random. Your goal is to move from that point along the curve to the highest point possible.

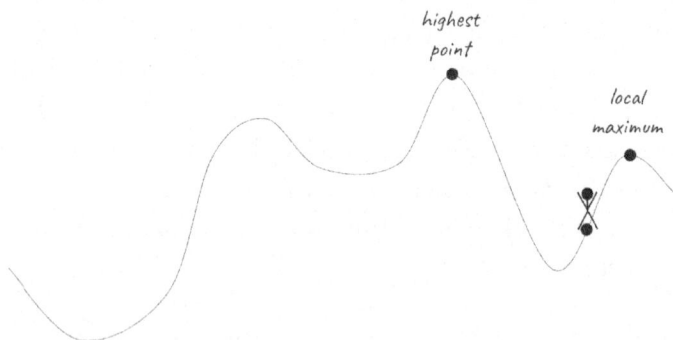

But there's a catch. You have to imagine that you literally *are* the dot on the curve. From the point of view of the dot, you don't have the luxury of seeing where the highest point on the entire curve is. You can only see what's immediately to your left or to your right. Your goal is to seek the highest point, so you go in the direction that's incrementally higher – in this case to the right.

Depending on where you start, you can get stuck at a local maximum instead of finding the *globally* best outcome. To find the hill with the highest peak, sometimes you need to go downhill for a bit. Sometimes you have to endure many low valleys in order to find the top of the highest mountain.

To see what's globally best, you need to zoom out. Rather than be a point on a line looking only to the left and to the right, you need to get far enough away to where you can see the big picture. Settling down at the top of a small hill when there are true mountains out there can be very limiting.

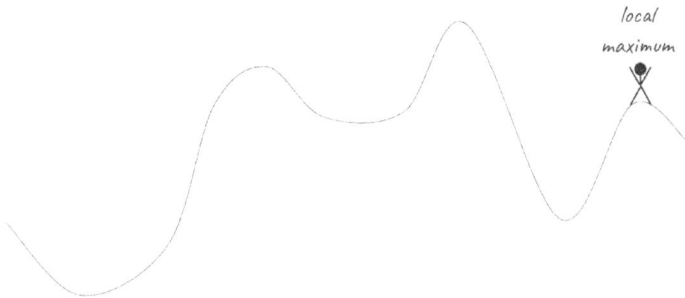

local
maximum

When decisions are based on the current situation, they are often incremental in nature. Most of us make decisions based on the options in front of us: left or right, up or down. Beware of making decisions this way, because incremental decisions lead to incremental outcomes. Sometimes you've got to zoom out to see where you want to end up. It may be more challenging to get off the hill you're on and transplant yourself near the highest mountain. But that's where you'll find the biggest rewards.

Saying "zoom out" is easy. But having a structured approach to vision and insight requires work. In the next sections, we'll get into how you can do it.

Vision & Insight

> *There are these two young fish swimming along, and they happen to meet an older fish swimming the other way, who nods at them and says, "Morning, boys. How's the water?" And the two young fish swim on for a bit, and then eventually one of them looks over at the other and goes, "What the hell is water?"*
> *– David Foster Wallace, American novelist*

> *In basketball they say, "You can't coach height," meaning all the coaching in the world won't make a player taller. It's almost as hard to teach insight.*
> *– Howard Marks, The Most Important Thing*

The Merriam Webster dictionary defines *vision* as "the act or power of seeing". That is the everyday, pedestrian definition. The follow-on definitions are more useful to us:

1. the act or power of *imagination*

2. a mode of seeing or *conceiving*; and,
3. unusual *discernment* or *foresight*

When we're talking about product vision, we're talking about the latter three definitions. We're referring to "conceiving" of something that is not there yet, but is possible. Looking at what is actual and seeing what is possible requires the power of imagination. Often it requires playing out how the future may unfold with the limited information available today – and that's *foresight*.

Visionaries see a possible future as clearly as day, and inspire others to see it too. Product managers need to take vision one step further. Product managers must also plot out the path from today's state to the end state, then lead the team to get from point A to B.

A close cousin to vision is *insight*. While vision is about seeing, *insight* is literally about seeing inward. Merriam Webster defines *insight* as:

1. the ability to understand people and situations in a very clear way
2. an understanding of the true nature of something; and,
3. the act or result of apprehending the inner nature of things or of seeing intuitively

Whereas vision is seeing something that is not there, insight is seeing what *is* there but which others don't see. Insightful people see what's in plain sight, but which others have overlooked or taken for granted.

31

Insight often involves putting together assets you already have in novel ways to get outcomes that, in hindsight, are obvious. Or finding a way to do much more, with less. Insight often leads to what looks like shortcuts.

People often say, "Teach me how to have vision!" Unfortunately, both insight and vision are hard to teach. They are muscles that must be built over a long time. When someone goes to the gym for the first time and attempts to lift weights, their muscles are not familiar with the movements. Arms tremble under the unfamiliar strain of exercise. After the workout, there is pain, yet no visible change to the muscles. Only after lots of training does the exercise begin to feel natural and the muscles begin to visibly develop.

So too it is with building the muscles of insight and vision. They come only with lots of practice trying on strange ideas and lots of coming up empty. To have vision, you have to think about possibilities from multiple angles, many of which will lead nowhere. You have to look into the future. You have to break things down and put them back together in new ways.

Insight often requires a deep understanding of a domain. And then, it requires having an open mind and a healthy habit of constantly questioning everything that is assumed to be true or unchangeable. What if some dogmas could be challenged and everything could be changed?

Vision is not about incremental changes. Having vision means seeing a version of the world that doesn't exist yet. In the language of hill climbing, vision is not about moving slightly to the left or slightly to the right. Vision means you can imagine yourself on a completely different mountain that is out of your current view.

Insight is about discerning something "obvious" that everyone else around hasn't seen yet. That makes the job more difficult: you've got to explain your insight to everyone in such a way that it seems obvious once they've heard your pitch – but without it being so simplistic that it seems foolish. "If it's so simple and obvious, why hasn't it already been done?"

Is your vision big enough?

How big does your vision need to be? Here it's useful to distinguish between a company's mission and vision, and a product vision.

A company's mission, often codified in a "mission statement", is a general statement of an organization's purpose. It's usually *intentionally* not actually achievable and therefore almost never has to change.

A company vision will be more constrained. A company vision describes an achievable goal that fits under the mission, and can actually be delivered in finite time – even if it takes a very long time.

Your *product* vision may be one and the same as the company vision. It should describe a product that can be developed by engineers based on a spec and delivered on a schedule. It still may take multiple years and many releases of intermediate steps until the complete vision is fully achieved.

Tesla's mission statement is "to accelerate the world's transition to sustainable energy." Notice how this statement is about an ongoing and perhaps never-ending process.

A specific product vision within Tesla might have been "An all-electric luxury sedan that can drive from Boston to New York City on a single charge." The realization of that vision would have been the Tesla Model S.

Depending on where you are in your company's evolution, the company vision and product vision may be one and the same. However, when a company wants to broadcast a huge ambition, the mission statement may be so general that it can support a number of enduring missions. In fact, Tesla is a case in point, and their mission statement evolved over time.

Tesla's original mission was not "to accelerate the world's transition to sustainable energy," but "to accelerate the world's transition to sustainable transport". At the time that statement was adopted, "transport" was probably thought to be sufficiently broad as to drive decades of the company's work. Because "transport" encompassed more than just cars, there was headroom for expanding into other methods of transportation, like planes, trains, boats and rocket ships. But the mission statement didn't account for other use cases of energy, generally speaking. In 2016, Tesla changed its mission to be agnostic to the energy use case, and Tesla now sells solar roofs, which have nothing to do with transport.

To balance Tesla's expansive mission, they have a company vision, "to create the most compelling car company of the 21st century by driving the world's transition to electric vehicles." This is a lot closer to their original mission statement, and is clearly achievable.

Product visions for individual Tesla cars are concrete, and each should fit under the hierarchy of their broad company mission and the company vision of "driving the world's transition to electric vehicles".

Frameworks & Tools to Innovate

There are a variety of ways to start training the muscle of vision and insight, and there are many techniques to unlock innovation. But they all lead back to the same place: the user. At the end of the day, if there is no user, then there is also no product.

Often people start with a technology, and trust that if they put a product out into the world, users will stumble upon it, figure out how to use it, and the rest will be history. But thinking like this simply does not offer the best chance of a product succeeding. What if the users for whom your product is a match never find it? Or what if it doesn't satisfy their actual needs or achieve product-market fit? Or what if they can't see how to adapt your product to their existing workflows?

Having a very clear idea of who your user is, understanding their problems, and *solving those problems* is the key to success. A user's needs may not always be technology gaps. Needs can be emotional, too. Sometimes all that it takes to win over customers is to make sure the product makes them feel the way they want to feel.

Frameworks that others have developed can help structure your thinking or help you think outside the box. In this section, I'll describe four such frameworks. First, I'll describe the Technology Adoption Life Cycle, famously described by Geoffrey Moore in his book, *Crossing the Chasm*. Second, I'll talk about the Jobs To Be Done framework created by Clayton Christensen. Third, I'll discuss the *Blue Ocean Strategy*, a book and set of tools developed by professors from INSEAD business school to help a business break out of the rut of competing in commodity markets. Finally, I'll highlight Doblin's Ten Types of Innovation, a framework created by Deloitte.

As you read through this section, think about how each of these frameworks applies to your situation and to your users.

Technology Adoption Life Cycle

In his book, *Crossing the Chasm*, Goeffrey Moore made famous the technology adoption life Cycle. Simply put, not everyone adopts technology in the same way. There is a spectrum of how people bring technology into their lives – from trying new things just for the sake of it to downright resisting anything new. I'll describe the five groups on the spectrum, then discuss why it's critical you know which group your product is best suited for today, and what it will take to appeal to groups further down the spectrum.

The five groups are Innovators, Early Adopters, Early Majority, Late Majority, and Laggers. The Innovators, Early Adopters represent the early market, and the Early Majority, Late Majority, and Laggers represent the mainstream market. There's a chasm between the early and mainstream markets, and you have to totally change how you package, deliver and market your product to cross that chasm.

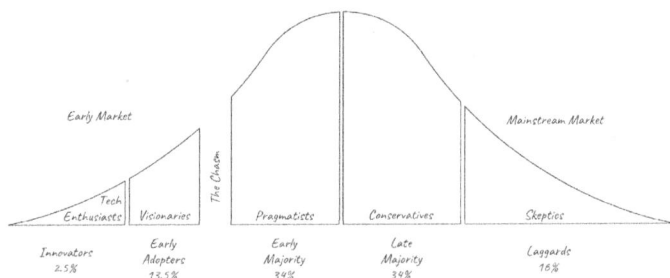

The Technology Adoption Life Cycle

Innovators

Innovators, or *tech enthusiasts*, will try something new simply *because* it's new. They buy the latest gadgets even if they don't have a clear notion of how they'll use that product in their life. People in this group were the first to buy drones when they were expensive, noisy, and ran out of batteries quickly. They were the first to have VR headsets. You get the idea.

This group is technologically savvy, and enjoys spending their disposable income on gadgets.

The Innovators group represents only 2.5% of the population. If your product only suits innovators, you may not have much of a market. But they're an important segment when a technology is so new that it has a very high price point, and when the technology is not yet mature enough to live up to many of its promises.

Early Adopters

Like Innovators, Early Adopters are also technologically savvy. However, they don't buy new technology just for the sake of trying the latest gadget. What matters to the Early Adopter is that the product provides actual value by solving a real problem they have. Early Adopters, or *Visionaries*, can see how new products and services can be fit into their lives in beneficial ways, even when the product isn't specifically marketed that way, or designed to fully solve the problem.

When an Early Adopter sees a product that has potential, they'll take on efforts to fit that product into their life's workflow. This means a product that is relatively immature has a good shot with an Early Adopter. The product may not yet integrate easily with other products, and the Early Adopter will figure out how to integrate it themselves. The product may not have the best documentation or customer support yet, and the Early Adopter will be resourceful and figure things out on their own, or with the help of online forums.

The Early Adopter will make their purchase decision by

reading the specs of the product and doing their own online research. They're self-directed. Because they're okay with using bleeding edge products, they don't bother asking their friends what products they use; it's unlikely their network has even discovered the products that the Early Adopter is considering.

The Early Adopter group represents 13.5% of the population. New products that find success with this market segment, which is eager to try new things, may still face challenges reaching the mainstream market. The Early Adopter was willing to go the extra mile to get the product to work for them. But the segments in the mainstream market will do no such thing.

Early Majority

The Early Majority is the first group in the mainstream market. The Early Majority is full of *Pragmatists who* want to solve problems efficiently and with low risk. Unlike Early Adopters, who are tech savvy and delight in adapting new and unproven products into their lives, the pragmatic Early Majority wants a product that already has an established track record at solving problems just like their own.

More likely than not, the Early Majority will require that the product they select can integrate with everything else they already own. They won't be interested in spending precious hours building their own integrations or working out custom workflows to adapt your product into their life.

The way that a Pragmatist in the Early Majority learns about a product and makes a purchasing decision is by relying on others in their network for a reference. They actually want to see that people who they consider to be similar to them – who have the same problems and needs as they do – will vouch for your product. They're not interested in tech specs or marketing material. The Early Majority's main influence is through their network – primarily other discriminating Pragmatists who they know they can trust.

You can win over the Early Adopter market with a great product, but you need a different tactic to win over the early Majority. You won't win them over with more marketing. That's why there's a chasm between the Early Adopters and the Early Majority. Winning over the Early Majority requires two parallel activities. The first takes aim at their need for the product to fully fit into their life in a predictable and complete way. The second addresses the need to create solid references for your product within their like-minded group. Both of these represent a major change in how you position the product – and may require a significant amount of work.

To ensure a product fits into a Pragmatist's life, you need to think not only about the core technology product, but everything else you sell with it. Is there training available? Does it come with technical support? Does it integrate easily with an ecosystem of other products that the Pragmatist user is already likely to own?

Think of Apple products. For a long time, Apple was famous for making expensive computers that were used only by graphic designers. Macs weren't known for running all of the software that regular people needed. People outside of the creative arts viewed Apple products skeptically. Cheaper PCs running Windows were what pretty much everyone else used.

Then suddenly lots more people started using Macs. What happened? Apple addressed the needs of the early majority by wrapping Apple products in all the things Early Majority Pragmatists want. Apple ensured all of their products worked seamlessly together in an Apple ecosystem. Unlike finicky PCs, Macs had truly simple Plug & Play for hardware. Apple's software all worked seamlessly together – first with iLife and iWork, followed by iCloud to allow devices to connect seamlessly through the internet.

But tailoring to the Early Majority goes beyond the core product and its tech specs to all aspects of how users experience your product. For example, Apple started offering AppleCare. The Early Majority is full of pragmatists who need to know their product will be supported for as long as they own it. Knowing how critical customer support is, Apple branded it, and actually charges consumers a premium for AppleCare. Customers in the Early Majority are happy to pay up because predictable support is actually one of their purchase criteria.

Apple also opened Apple Stores. These stores aren't just a place to try and buy Apple products. Apple Stores have a Genius Bar, where anyone can get support for their Apple products in person from a smart, friendly Apple Store employee. Many Apple Stores also host free classes where you can learn how to use your Mac, or how to use the professional software sold in the Apple Store, like Final Cut Pro. For a would-be buyer who isn't familiar with Apple products and is worried they'll have trouble adapting, the presence of these classes offers reassurance that help is nearby.

The second need of the Early Majority is references from others like themselves. Moore's *Crossing the Chasm* suggests sub-segmenting the market into groups that can be one over one by one. For an example, think of the companies Dropbox and Box. These two companies create essentially the same product, and they have nearly identical names. How is it that they are both successful – and seemingly don't even compete with one another in the same market?

Both Dropbox and Box are online document storage solutions. Dropbox is a fairly generic product, and it's great at what it does – store files. Most online services that *can* integrate with online file storage solutions *do* integrate with Dropbox. Lots of people use it.

But for a company with specific enterprise needs, Box is a better fit. Box took aim at solving enterprise problems and making it clear to their target market that they had solved those problems and had done so completely. While both products integrate with just about everything, Box makes a point of integrating with tools used by enterprises, like popular CRMs. While both have high privacy standards, Box goes a step further by allowing enterprise customers to utilize their own security keys. They've achieved security standards allowing them to store data for organizations in regulated industries such as government and healthcare.

From the outside, it may seem like Box and Dropbox simply built their products for different segments from Day 1 – enterprise versus consumer. But in reality, it took concerted effort for Box to tailor their product for one enterprise segment at a time. They had to understand that segment's needs fully and build all the glue and support pieces needed and expected by that segment, and then win the segment over. Once they had happy customers within an industry, those customers could serve as reference points for others in the same industry who wanted a proof point that Box could address their complex needs.

The Early Majority represents 34% of the market. As such, they're an important group to break into to continue your product's growth. But as you can see, it takes a lot of work beyond simply building the core technology product to win over these Pragmatists.

Late Majority

The Late Majority, or Conservatives, do not jump into a product until the market is very mature. They prefer a solution they already know works to anything new. On top of that, they are price sensitive.

A Late Majority user views making a change in their workflow as an inconvenient burden. They typically will not adapt their behavior until it's less convenient to do things the old way than to switch to the new way. For example, while Early Majority users were using apps to call Ubers and Lyfts, Late Majority users were still calling a telephone number to schedule a taxi, or searching for taxi stands. After some tipping point, it became hard to find a taxi in many cities. Once literally everybody was using Uber or Lyft, Late Majority users finally gave in and figured out how to use those apps, too.

Late Majority users also typically wait for the price of a product to come down before they'll consider buying it. They won't pay a premium for *newness* or bells and whistles. The Late Majority will be perfectly happy to buy the cheaper, plastic version of your product. Only when a product is extremely mature and the cost of production has come down does it make sense to spend any money marketing toward the Late Majority. They're also a perfect audience for the "N-1" version of your product, also known as "last year's model". When the latest numbered iPhone is released and all of the Early Adopters rush out to get it, the Late Majority will happily buy the budget iPhone SE at a deep discount.

The Late Majority group represents another sizable 34% of the market. But don't bother going after this segment until your product is mature and costs have come way down.

Laggards

Laggards are the final group and make up about 16% of the market. You can't market to them directly, because they delight in *not* buying your product. They will only use it when they have no other choice.

For example, a Laggard would never think to buy a digital camera. But for many years now, safety laws have required all new cars to have back-up cameras. Once a Laggard finds themselves buying one of these cars – probably much later than everyone else – they also have no choice but to buy the digital camera that comes embedded in it.

Directly embedding or bundling your product with another product that people are already buying is a great way to get through to pretty much all segments. Just think of the snack brands offered for free on flights. They certainly aren't the best. You'd never seek them out on your own. But these subpar options are the only option for the hundreds of millions passengers taking flights each year. By striking a deal with the airline, the snackmaker virtually guarantees their success for years.

Lessons from Crossing the Chasm

It's critical to remember that not all users are the same, and especially that not all users are like you.

Understanding how "complete" your product offering is in terms of overall polish, breadth of integrations, documentation and support, and industry-specific solutions will help you identify what segment of the technology adoption life Cycle your target user is in. Where they are will heavily influence your current marketing plan.

Having this framework at your fingertips will also help you understand what you have to do to break into segments further down the adoption curve.

Jobs to be Done

In his book *Competing Against Luck*, Clayton Christensen described a new theory of product innovation called "Jobs to be Done". The core premise of Jobs to be Done is that customers have specific outcomes they need in their lives, and they "hire" tools and services to achieve those outcomes – to "get the job done."

A colleague of Christensen's at Harvard Business School, Theodore Levitt, said, "People don't want to buy a quarter-inch drill. They want a quarter-inch hole!" Often product designers come to the table with the task of building a better proverbial mousetrap. But customers don't want a "better mousetrap," they want to eradicate mice. In other words, in *Jobs to be Done*, the focus shifts from the tool to the outcome. While tools may be ephemeral, the outcomes people seek in their lives tend to be stable and transcend today's offerings of tools.

Think of automobiles. If your job was to innovate in the space of automobiles, you might start by thinking of the characteristics of automobiles and how you could optimize them: make the car faster, quieter, more fuel efficient, etc. But optimizing the tool misses the point that the *job* of the automobile is to get the user from one place to another, safely and comfortably. Remember the quote famously attributed to Henry Ford, "If I had asked people what they wanted, they would have said faster horses." Knowing your target user, what job they need to get done, and where today's products are falling short helps focus where you can innovate.

Since Ford's day, cars and their production have been optimized in every way imaginable. After the latest technological innovations fully take hold – electric motors and self-driving capabilities – the problem of getting someone from one place to another could be considered pretty well solved. But that won't mean there's nothing left to do. Buyers of automobiles actually have more Jobs to be Done for which they hire cars than simply getting people from one place to another. And that's why we have different kinds of automobiles.

Did you know that the best selling "car" in the United States for more than 40 years is actually the Ford F-150 *truck*? A truck does a different job than a typical passenger car. It not only gets people from one place to another; it also transports construction materials and other bulky items.

Cars serve another job these days as well. People spend a lot of time in cars, such that cars are becoming thought of as a third space apart from home and the workplace. Luxury vehicle manufacturers have been capitalizing on this "third space" metaphor, adapting cars to be more like extensions of the home. For example, video entertainment systems now occupy kids in the backseat. Cars with such systems satisfy an additional job, "Keep the kids occupied."

Once self-driving cars become a reality, drivers won't be preoccupied with the task of driving at all. They'll hire cars for new tasks, like providing a productive working space during the commute to work. At that point we're likely to see a car's front seats face inward rather than forward, tables in the center of the car, and proper outlets for laptops.

How can you spot innovation opportunities in the Jobs to be Done framework? In a customer interview, have users describe their entire workflows. Rather than focus on the individual elements of their current solution, seek to understand the outcomes they're after. When you spot workarounds that users have crafted *around* today's tools to get to their outcomes, you have an insight into what kind of end-to-end solution may be required.

In Christensen's original book, he described a fast food chain that hired his team to boost milkshake sales. The chain had tried everything they could think of, but had been focusing on the quality of the milkshake itself: it's taste, mouth feel, etc., but to no avail.

Through customer interviews, Christensen's team spotted the job people were hiring milkshakes for: to give them something to do on their commute to work and keep them satiated for the entire morning through to lunch. A milkshake was better than a banana, which was consumed too quickly and left the user hungry by the end of the commute. It was also better than a bagel or breakfast sandwich that might leave crumbs or make your hands sticky. The milkshake was easy to consume in the car over a long period of time because cars come with cup holders where the milkshake can sit between sips.

With this insight into the job that customers hired the milkshake to do, Christensen's team was able to make recommendations that helped the milkshake do that specific job even better. They suggested packaging that allowed bigger milkshakes to fit in the same-sized cup holders in cars. They suggested thickening the milkshake and adapting the straw so the milkshake would take longer to consume. And they suggested special drive through lanes for morning milkshake buyers who just wanted to get their milkshake quickly and get on the road.

Christensen's *Competing Against Luck* was published in 2016. There have been many formulations since that put the Jobs to be Done framework to work in your organization by systematizing the process of using it. Now that you know the concept at a high level, you can start using it immediately, or dive deeper into other resources if you need more structure.

Blue Ocean Strategy

Blue Ocean Strategy, by W. Chan Kim, Renee Mauborgne, et al., is an invaluable book about market positioning. If your product is largely a commoditized good, this book presents six paths to adapting your product to create a totally new market and attract an entirely new audience.

In a commoditized market, companies fight over the same customers with very similar products. The way to win is to offer more of the product, for less money. It's a bloody fight to zero margins – a red ocean. The authors suggest that you can reframe your product and create an entirely new adjacent market free from competition – a blue ocean.

As with Crossing the Chasm's focus on market segments, often your core product doesn't change when you target a new segment, but how you deliver it does.

Path 1 is to focus on alternatives rather than competitors. In the streaming wars, you might think Netflix's competitors are Disney Plus, Hulu, and Amazon Prime. And on some very real level, they are, today. But Reed Hastings, Netflix founder and CEO, famously said that Netflix is actually competing with sleep. That's a powerful observation that led Netflix to a different Go-to-Market strategy for their product. The norm on network TV had previously been to release shows serially, one episode per week. Netflix was the first streaming service to drop an entire series in one go. These drops resulted in binge watching, with customers glued to their screens late into the night until they couldn't keep their eyes open any longer. Rather than suggest viewers turn off the TV and come back next week, Netflix autoplays the next episode within seconds after the current one ends.

Today Netflix's competitors look more and more like Netflix, owing to Netflix's success in creating a new market space. Network created this space, not by doing what TV was already doing, but better. No, they created an alternative to sleep. And until everyone other streaming services caught up, they printed money.

Path 2 is to look across strategic groups in an industry. All airlines sell airplane seats and get you from point A to B – but a flight on Southwest is targeted at flyers on a budget while seats in United's Polaris class are targeted at business travelers with large expense accounts. Tailoring an offering to a very specific audience can help gain that audience's loyalty. Gyms targeted at women are another example. Arguably these gyms have cut their potential membership in half, but in reality, they are so much more appealing to their target audience than standard gyms that they more than make up for the smaller addressable market size.

Path 3 is to rethink who makes the decision to buy. For some products, the end user and the buyer are the same person. But very often, they are different people. For example, almost everything that's for a child is purchased by a parent. While the child wants an item to be interesting and fun and come in shiny packaging, a parent wants the item to be long-lasting and safe, and perhaps also educational.

For enterprise goods, there are often three types of people in the equation. Consider a tool used on a factory floor to accomplish a task. The end user actually uses the tool and needs it to be of high quality and do the job well. There are also life cycle participants who install and maintain the tool, and potentially train the workers in how the tool works. And the financial or buying participants decide which tool to buy, from whom, and how to finance it. While often we only think of innovating for the end user, often there's a lot of potential to unlock in innovating for users who participate in the product at other stages. Can you make your product easier to maintain or provide service contracts, and market directly to the life cycle participants? Can you make it easier to finance and market to the back-office folks?

Path 4 is to look at complementary products and service offerings. Could your product be improved by bundling in other products and services that are needed to get the full job done? As with the *Jobs to be Done* framework, think about why customers need your product in the first place. If your product doesn't solve the customer's problem until they find and buy other products and services first, then you have room to improve your offering. This can mean bundling hardware and software together, or any subscriptions that may be needed to make full use of your product. A simple example here is toys that have "batteries included." Who wants to deal with the let down of a child unwrapping a gift on Christmas, only to realize that batteries are needed to operate the toy and none are around?

Path 5 is to rethink the functional-emotional spectrum. While some people prefer to buy products based on technical specs – think *Early Adopters* from the Technology Adoption Life Cycle – others are more likely to buy when the product promises to solve a problem and make them feel better. For example, a VPN may have a lot of technical features that a techie would want to compare across competing products. But a non-techie just wants to *feel safe*.

A massage is just a massage, right? A sports massage and a "deep tissue" spa treatment are essentially the same thing, but the former feels clinical and functional, while the latter feels luxurious and pampering. It's the same activity, but it feels like a completely different product. It's more likely that the sports massage practitioner will talk to you during the treatment, while the deep tissue massage therapist will play relaxing music and scent the air with soothing fragrances. Extend this example with Path 4; you'd choose different complementary products to bundle with each, too. You might bundle a muscle rolling ball with the sport massage, while the massage at the spa might come with an hour in the plunge pools and cucumber-infused water.

Path 6 is to think about how to shape trends rather than to merely respond to them. The world is not a static place. As the famous hockey player Wayne Gretzky said, "skate to where the puck is going to be, not where it has been." No one wants to be in a reactive mode all the time. Take a step back and think about where your industry is headed. Who are the players, what are they doing, and more importantly, what are they likely to do next? If you know your industry well, you can predict where you need to be. While everyone else is catching up to you, you can be in a position to shape the trend, not merely to respond to it. Typically having adequate size or adequate funding (or both) is a prerequisite to shaping a trend.

Doblin's Ten Types of Innovation

The final framework I'll mention, and just briefly, is Doblin's Ten Types of Innovation. Doblin, a Deloitte company, has broken down innovation into ten categories. They are described in the book, *Ten Types of Innovation*, by Larry Keeley, Ryan Pikkel, et al., and on their website, http://doblin.com/ten-typ es.

The ten types break down into three categories: Configuration, Offering, and Experience. Configuration innovation relates to the inner workings of the company – its profit model, how it interoperates with business partners, the internal structure of the business, and internal processes. The Offering category relates to the core product and the system of interconnected products meant to be used together. Finally, the Experience category relates to the services offered in conjunction with the product, the channels through which you can get the product offering, how the offering is branded, and how the company engages with its customers.

In addition to the book and website, Doblin offers a pack of 100 cards that act as innovation prompts. These cards can be used to drive brainstorming sessions within your organization by challenging you to think about your company, offering, or experience in different ways.

As you might guess, there's a lot of overlap between all of these frameworks. The Jobs to be Done framework fits almost entirely into the *Offering* category of Doblin's Ten Types. And Doblin's Experience category maps to Blue Ocean Strategy's functional-emotional spectrum.

It's not so much that one framework is right and the others are wrong, or that you need to pick one. Each framework stresses different aspects of innovation, which may be more or less important depending on the maturity of your product and market and the stage of growth of your business. For now it's good to have an overview of each, and you can dive deeper into them when you sense your product is facing one of the challenges that they're intended to address.

3

The Product Development Life Cycle

The product development life cycle has distinct stages, and different parts of the team will be involved in each stage. Although many teams and individuals will be doing the actual work of building and launching the product, the PM acts as the glue that holds it together, ensuring everyone is aligned and executing toward the shared goal.

The following diagram shows a summary of the product life cycle, starting with *Alignment* activities, followed by *Execution* activities leading to launch, and finally the *Post-launch* activities. Throughout this chapter, I'll go into detail on what happens in each stage, who's involved, and what key artifacts help the team get their work done. The make everything extremely clear, I'll:

- explain the *purpose* of the phase
- outline who your *partners* are during that phase
- explain the *activities* that should be undertaken
- describe the *artifacts* that should be created.

If your organization doesn't already have a process in place, you can take the lead in defining one, using this chapter as a template.

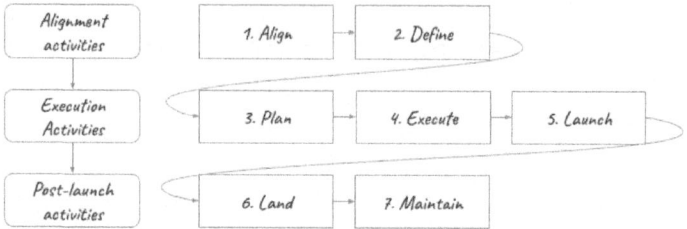

The stages of the product development life cycle

Phase 1: Align

Cheat sheet: Align

Purpose
    The purpose of the Align phase is to gain agreement on the high-level problem to be solved, an idea of the business outcomes sought, and a rough solution.

Partners
    Business stakeholders, tech and UX lead, and cross-functional partners

Activities
  Market research, brainstorming, visioning work, fitting solutions to the problem and opportunities

Artifacts
  2-pager, by the PM
  Vision deck, by the PM
  UX concepts & wireframes, by UX
  Roadmap, by the PM

Validation
  Market research, by Marketing or the PM
  User needs research, by UXR

Purpose

Before a team starts working on a project in earnest, there's meta-work required to determine what is going to be done, and why. The purpose of the Align phase is to gain agreement on the high-level problem to be solved, an idea of the business outcomes sought, and a rough solution. In addition to coming up with the proposal, the whole team needs to be bought in.

The visionary product direction may be too broad or too big for the team to work on in a single go. The Product Manager and her engineering and UX counterparts need to break it down into something more tractable to start – a minimum viable product, or *MVP* – that is the first step on the journey to the complete vision, and show the roadmap for how the full vision will eventually be realized.

Partners

Business stakeholders need to be bought into the problem, opportunity and solution in order to greenlight the project. Looping them into the process from the start ensures where you intend to take the team is in line with their expectations, goals, and bigger-picture plans.

Engineering lead (aka, the tech lead) and a UX lead are critical thought partners during this stage for exploring the problem space and working out potential solutions. During this phase, the UX can rapidly create low-fidelity wireframes to demonstrate how the potential solutions might take shape. The tech lead consults on what is possible.

Cross-functional partners like marketing, sales, and even customer support can be invaluable in this stage as well. They regularly hear from customers and can provide valuable insights that guide the solutions space.

Activities

During the Align phase, you'll meet with the partners listed above. Your goal is to open up the solution space, test out ideas rapidly, and then quickly narrow down to proposals for what the team will ultimately pursue. Use the 2-pager described in the Artifacts section as a guide for the type of information you'll want to collect to make your case.

Artifacts

The key artifacts of the Align stage serve as a communication medium to explain the product plan to your main stakeholders – upwards, laterally and down. The product manager creates product briefs and vision decks, and a rough roadmap of when the proposed product could be delivered. The UX team creates wireframes and rough mocks that get an idea across of what's possible.

A 2-pager or product brief

The 2-pager, or product brief, is a quick document that you can share with others. It allows you to get your product direction ideas across succinctly. It's a 1,000-10,000 foot view of the problem and opportunity and the proposed product. The 2-pager sets up the context required for the eng team to understand what they are building and why, but isn't detailed enough to actually describe what is to be built.

The PM should take the lead in writing the 2-pager to socialize the product idea with the team. Feedback is essential to adapt the idea before making lots of additional investments in other artifacts. The 2-pager should cover these key areas:

- Problem statement
- Opportunity
- Strategy for attacking the problem
- High level wireframes or mocks of the user experience
- High level description of what components must be built
- Key success metrics

- Validation plan
- Rough milestones
- Risks that may hinder success

A 2-pager template with more details on each prompt is available in the *Tools of the Trade* chapter.

A 2-pager is a lot like the introduction to a Product Requirements Document (PRD) that will be written in the *Define* phase, and often it will guide your development of your PRD. The full PRD is where you'll go into specific detail for the engineering team. Before getting so detailed, you want to be sure the team is aligned on the idea.

Vision deck

A vision deck and a 2-pager share a lot in common, but the vision deck will often cover more aspects about the viability of the product proposal, including a more detailed view of business opportunity and a Go-To-Market strategy. By nature of being in a presentation format, the vision deck lends itself to being shared with and presented to stakeholders, leadership, and executives. You'll create a vision deck once the team has aligned around the ideas presented in the 2-pager and is ready to go deeper into the proposed solution space.

Here are some topics to cover in a vision deck:

- What problem are you solving, or what opportunity are you capitalizing on?
- What is the value proposition for the user?

- How will you solve the problem? Is there a high level snapshot of the user experience that can get the product idea across?
- What alternatives exist? Why don't they meet user needs?
- What is the business model?
- What are the financial projections?
- What is the go-to-market strategy?
- What are the risks?
- What does the rough roadmap / timeline look like?

While the PM is the "owner" of the deck, the PM should rely on the cross-functional team to pull together all of the necessary information. There are many considerations and advisors or partners you'll want to include in the early stages as consultants in order to build the best proposal. The marketing team can help understand market dynamics and think through Go-To-Market strategy. User Experience Designers can speak to the complexity of making a product usable. Engineering leads can help you understand what's technically possible. Lawyers can tell you what your legal risks are.

The 2-pager and vision deck may incorporate UX wireframes or rough mocks that get across an idea of the product. At this stage, visuals are more about creating a high level feeling about what's possible than showing specific flows or user interactions. While not concrete, a picture is nonetheless worth a thousand words and can ensure everyone in your audience is on the same page.

Roadmap

The roadmap is a high level timeline. The roadmap starts with where you are now, and it ends with your vision being realized, with rough dates. The roadmap shows how the first delivery, the MVP or *minimum viable product*, fits into the bigger picture.

In a roadmap, key outcomes and milestones should be roughly fixed to future dates, coming to an ultimate conclusion. When possible, link the roadmap to key external dates, such as release cycles you need to confirm to, marketing moments, or other important dates for your organization. For example, if building tax software for the US market, Jan 1 and April 14 would be critical dates to reflect in your roadmap.

The roadmap describes milestones or key delivered work, not individual work items. Typically roadmaps are high level enough that the scale should be months, quarters or years – not days or weeks. Individual work items, which may be measured in days or weeks, do not belong in a roadmap, but in a project plan, described in *Phase 3: Execute*.

A roadmap is a key tool for large long-range product development. During that time, your sponsors and stakeholders may forget why your project is so important, especially when new competing opportunities come up. You will be asked, "When can we free up the engineers working on your project?" When you get this question, you can bring everyone's attention back to the roadmap. It shows not just the current work, but the next work that needs to follow in order to realize the complete product vision.

Validation

Validation during the *Align* phase consists of ensuring you're on the right track: that there's a space in the market for your product, and that users want it.

The two most useful types of research in this phase are market research and user needs research. Often you can find market research on your own, or your marketing team may be a great resource.

User needs research may also be done by the marketing team, or may be undertaken by a User Experience Research team. I discuss both of these types of research in the *Validation* chapter.

Phase 2: Define

Cheat sheet: Define

Purpose
   The purpose of the Define stage is to define the product in detail so the engineering team knows what needs to be built, and the cross-functional team can start planning around the new product. The engineering team should start designing the product implementation.

Partners
   User experience designer, Engineering lead, User experience researcher, XFN partners

Activities
Sessions to walk the team through the product definition, gather feedback and adjust

Artifacts
A Product Requirements Document (PRD), by the PM
Technical design, by the TL
UX mocks, by the PM

Validation
User experience research, by UXR

Purpose

Once there's high-level alignment on the problem and proposed solution, the product needs to be defined in detail. Whereas the Align stage identifies the opportunity, the high level goals and a rough idea of the product that would meet those goals, the Define stage gets very specific as to what product will be built to achieve the goal.

Partners

User experience designer, Engineering lead, User experience researcher, XFN partners

Activities

In this stage the product manager writes a Product Requirements Document (PRD) that completely describes the product to be built and its behavior under all circumstances. To support this detailed definition, the UX designer will create a complete set of rough mocks showing all of the product flows for the product's user journeys.

The PM and the UX designer work collaboratively and in tandem as the mocks and PRD are fleshed out. Typically the PM will host sessions to walk the working team of engineers and cross-functional stakeholders through the product definition. This provides an opportunity to gather feedback, uncover overlooked areas of definition and adjust until the product definition feels complete.

With an understanding of the user journeys and the product requirements from the PRD and the UX mocks, the engineering team authors an engineering design document that describes the technical architecture, dependencies, schemas, APIs, and technology modules that will be created to deliver the product.

This PRD written by the product manager should be detailed enough for all cross-functional teams to understand how the product will behave and start planning their work around it. For example, the QA team may begin thinking about their test plans at this stage, and the marketing team can start a Go-To-Market plan, though they may also wait until execution begins.

Artifacts

The key artifacts of the Define stage serve as blueprints that help the whole team do their work during Execution. The product team creates Product Requirement Documents (PRDs) describing how the product must behave. The UX team creates mocks of the complete product experience describing how the product will look and be experienced by users. And the engineering team writes a technical design document describing how the product will be built.

Product Requirements Document (PRD)

If there is a central document core to the art of Product Management, it is the PRD. The PRD is an invaluable tool for getting their teams focused on a singular objective.

The product requirements document (PRD) explains why it's important to solve this problem and build the product. It describes for whom the product is designed and exactly what they can do with the product.

The PRD is an essential document. It should be written as early in the process as is practical, and everyone on the team should become intimately familiar with it. It's incumbent on the product manager to walk the entire product team through the document – multiple times if necessary – until everyone agrees the document accurately describes the team's shared vision.

The rest of the team will base their work on the PRD. The

user experience team (UX) will propose mocks for the product experience flows that accomplish the user goals and objectives defined in the PRD, and they will be incorporated into the PRD itself.

The engineering team will use the PRD as a basis for the *technical design document,* which describes how the software will be designed to accomplish the needs set forth within the PRD.

The QA team will develop their test plans based on the capabilities and use-cases described in the PRD.

The Customer Service team will start planning for new help content and scripts for agents. So on and so forth.

The PRD should always be the source of truth of the product definition, so the product manager must keep it up to date whenever product decisions change during the product development process. In that sense, the PRD is a living document. Whenever a consequential change is made, the product manager should get the word out – getting the team together if needed to review the changed requirements to ensure everyone is on the same page.

In the Tools of the Trade section, I dive deep into the details of what goes into a PRD. By understanding what's in it, you'll get a better sense of the work that has to happen during this phase.

Validation

Once the UX mocks have been developed, they can be put in front of users to ensure the experience is understandable and usable. See the *Validation* chapter for a deeper explanation of user experience research.

Note that a formal study of the user experience is not always required, and is often skipped if the product changes are incremental in nature and non-controversial.

When all parties are aligned that the product is achieving the right goals via the PRD, that the user experience described by the UX mocks accomplish the goals and pass usability testing, and that the technical design elegantly satisfies the requirements, then it's time to move on to the *Plan* phase.

Phase 3: Plan

Planning can sound boring, but it's critical. Consider these questions:

1. Are you able to foresee business and engineering dependencies and plan ahead accordingly?
2. Are you able to negotiate and coordinate with other teams?
3. Can you communicate your plan effectively throughout the organization to ensure everyone is bought into your timeline?

These are critical skills that you'll employ during this phase to get the actual work off on the right foot.

> ### Cheat sheet: Plan
>
> *Purpose*
> *The purpose of the Plan phase is to translate the product definition and technical design into a work plan and staffing picture that results in an estimation of when the product will be completed.*
>
> *Partners*
> *Project manager, Engineering manager, QA lead, Cross-team and external partners*
>
> *Activities*
> *Task enumeration, Effort estimation, Staffing allocation, Aligning to external calendars*
>
> *Artifacts*
> *Project plan, by the Project Manager or PM*
> *An approvals plan, by the Project Manager or PM*
> *QA test plan, by the QA team*
> *Staffing plan, by the engineering manager*

Purpose

The purpose of the *Plan* phase is to translate the product definition and technical design into a work plan that results in an estimation of when the product will be completed. Key timing issues that impact the launch or the ability to capitalize on the opportunity are accounted for now; for example, holiday shopping seasons. Cross-team and external dependencies will be accounted for now, such as when other teams can deliver inputs, or when launch partners deploy the launch vehicles that the team's software is contained within. To avoid any surprises, the team should work out a complete list of what approvals will be needed, whether from stakeholders, partners, or internal governance teams. This phase results in timelines, key milestones and an idea of who will be staffed on the project.

Partners

Project manager, Engineering manager, QA lead, Cross-team and external partners

Activities

In this phase, you'll work with the engineering tech lead and project manager to lay out a full plan with as much detail as you have available for all the activities you have insight into. Of course, this will be an iterative process, and you'll learn more about what needs to be done as you get deeper into the project. But writing down what you know early allows you to start planning for the approximate time when you can launch.

Once the engineering work is understood, engineering management can come up with a staffing plan — actually assigning engineers to work on the implementation.

Artifacts

Project plan

To make the execution phase successful, you'll need to have a project plan that breaks the work down into specific deliverables. What goes into a project plan? At its most basic level, the project plan is a list of things to be done – it's a checklist. The level of granularity is up to you. If you're working from a PRD, you might list all of the user journeys and all of the components from the requirements section.

You may also account for deliverables from the cross-functional team like the marketing plan and customer support plan in a project plan, but often it's cleaner to have a separate tracker for high level XFN tasks versus lower level engineering tasks. XFN deliverables are more likely to be tracked by the product manager than the project manager throughout the project.

The team will use the project plan as their guide throughout the project, reminding you on a daily basis what still needs to be done. At some regular cadence – typically weekly or bi-weekly if working in sprints – the project plan should be updated by the team to reflect work that has been completed, as well as any new work items that have come up.

In the Tools of the Trade section, I go into detail regarding exactly what goes into a project plan. Free to jump there now to get a sense for it before moving on.

THE PRODUCT MANAGER'S GUIDE

Approvals plan

An approvals plan should list the approvals needed and who is on point to give each approval. Approvers should typically not be contributors to the project, but instead be individuals who have oversight over many projects and can ensure consistency and adherence to policy across the company's products. The exception is a QA lead, who signs off that QA has passed. A typical list might include:

- Product leadership
- Engineering leadership
- Legal and risk
- Compliance teams such as security & privacy and regulator auditors
- QA for user acceptance testing

Often it's a good idea to get approvals in two stages. The first stage is as early as possible, ideally before execution begins in order to ensure the product definition and technical design satisfy any requirements the approvers will have.

The second and final approval is before launch, and is a final check that the actual product that was built still falls within the approved guidelines.

QA test plan

With the product behavior defined in the PRD, the QA team can begin putting together a list of test cases. As the engineering team delivers working components during the Execution phase, the QA team can begin to apply their plan and work toward a bug-free launch.

Staffing plan

It may seem obvious that once a project has been committed to, that it will be staffed. But staffing is actually not obvious at all. It's quite common for companies or teams to over-commit and assume that engineers or other staff can simply fit in another project after or around the other work they have on their plates already. It's a very conscientious team that accounts for their staff's time and takes care not to double book people.

During the planning phase is when you'll want to double check that you actually have peoples' time allocated to your project. Typically managers allocate the time of the people on their team. In addition to having people assigned, it's also critical to understand their priorities and whether your project is their main focus or one of many projects which they'll split their time between.

Validation

The main validation in the planning stage is whether the timeline for the solution fits the needs of the business. It may be the case that the desired feature set creates a timeline that is not tenable. In that case, it may be necessary to cut back part of the product feature set to bring in the timeline.

Governance partners may take issue with some part of the plan, which may also send the team back to the drawing board for some aspects of the product definition or the technical design.

Phase 4: Execute

> ### Cheat sheet: Execute
>
> *Purpose*
> *The Execution phase is when the engineering teams and all the individual contributors come into action to build out the actual product and all the supporting infrastructure.*
>
> *Partners*
> *Engineering team, QA team, Project manager*
>
> *Activities*
> *Engineering development, QA testing, tracking progress, and managing unforeseen circumstances*
>
> *Artifacts*
> *Status updates, by the PM or Project Manager*
>
> *Validation*

Dogfood results, by the PM
QA testing, by the QA team
User Acceptance Testing (UAT), by the QA team or PM

Purpose

Everything done before this phase was meta-work – the work of figuring out what the actual work will be. Here is the transition from meta-work to actual-work. Executing is the act of taking action and putting the wheels of your project in motion – doing the actual work. The Execution phase is when the engineering teams and all the individual contributors come into action to build out the actual product and all the supporting infrastructure.

Partners

Engineering team, QA team, Project managers

Activities

Engineering development

Engineering work is the most important activity in the company. The engineers actually build the product. Without the engineers there is nothing. They're an expensive resource so it's of the utmost importance to be sure they're working on the right things and that their work is in alignment with the company's goals. When the engineering team needs to backtrack or throw away work, it is incredibly costly.

How costly, you ask? Typically one product manager and one designer may work for a few months (up to 6 person-months) to define a product. Then ten to twenty engineers might work for 9 months or more to develop the product (up to 90-180 person-months). That's a huge disparity.

Almost everything done up to this point was to prepare for the engineering team to do their work with maximum efficiency.

There are many ways the engineering team can structure their development work. A popular choice these days is *agile*, but this term tends to mean different things to different people. That's in part because "agile" is an adjective describing the ability to move quickly and adapt, and in part because there are at least half a dozen forms of agile: scrum, lean, kanban, and more. Cottage industries of books, tools and workshops to teach the specifics of each of these methods and to bestow certifications like *Certified Scrum Master*. It can be overwhelming.

One of the main benefits of agile development is when the final goal of development is not clear to the stakeholders up front. Agile allows for constant changes of direction. As I've explained throughout the chapter, engineering is orders of magnitude more expensive than up-front design work. Most product design questions can be resolved by successive iterations of rapid design work versus costly weeks of engineering work. So it's no surprise that I don't recommend starting working when you don't have an end state in mind.

However, there are a handful of excellent practices from agile methods which are worth highlighting and keeping in your process. The first is to break work into short sprints, usually two weeks in length. Picking roughly two weeks of work at a time allows an opportunity to check in regularly to see if the team was able to deliver that work on schedule. If not, the schedule can be adjusted dynamically.

The second beneficial practice of agile methodologies is for the sprint outcome to be something that can be demonstrated to an audience. For example, in one method of development, a front-end developer and a back-end developer work in silos, developing two-weeks worth of code that isn't integrated. At the end of two weeks they each announce they're 10% complete with their respective work. Nothing is demonstrable, and you must take their word that they're 10% complete.

Alternatively, the team can structure the work so the front-end and back-end developers work together all along the way and deliver integrated work in every sprint. Even if the result of the first two weeks is a simple "Hello, world!", the fact that it's integrated has tremendous benefits. First, there's no blind faith required to understand what has or hasn't been completed because the team can see some functioning product, even if small. Second, the QA team can start testing the product throughout the development process. Third, integration work can be extremely time consuming and can easily throw off the timeline at the end of a project if it's saved for the end, so doing it all along the way derisks the project timeline.

The third beneficial practice is the demo. Having a ceremony that allows stakeholders to celebrate the engineering team's efforts can go a long way toward making the team feel valued. The demo also serves as a deadline that motivates the team to complete the sprint on time. Without such an internal deadline, it's easy for incomplete sprint-based work to get rolled over into the next sprint and allow the project to get off track.

Tracking progress

When you execute, the team finally devotes real time to building out the items in the work plan. During this time, the product manager or a project manager monitors progress. In smaller companies or on smaller projects, product managers double as project managers. In a bigger organization or company, a project manager may facilitate many aspects of the execution phase. The high level project plan developed in the *Plan* phase should be updated on a regular basis. If using an agile methodology, there may be another planning tool such as a Kanban board that will also be updated.

Managing unforeseen circumstances

As they say, ideas are a dime a dozen, and execution is everything. Having a project plan helps ensure the team has thought through everything that needs to happen in advance. But it won't be enough. Projects almost never go according to your project plan. Unforeseen tasks and unexpected surprises always arise. This gap between idea and execution is where product managers add tremendous value. The product manager's job is to help the team deliver on the vision. For example, how do you handle a surprise new requirement from the legal team? What if the launch date is tied to an important external event, but dogfooding reveals the product is not ready for launch?

Executing requires the team to parry and weave as they inevitably encounter problems and unexpected work. Product managers need to be resourceful, tenacious individuals who can help the team get the job done even in the face of unforeseen circumstances or surprise blockers. Executing well means finding a way to get the job done despite the circumstances that come up as you go, or adjusting expectations and the plan as needed to account for the unexpected. You've got to do whatever it takes to launch, pivot, or turn the project down gently. Product managers don't give up!

Ensuring visibility

Ensuring visibility to project sponsors, stakeholders and partners is critical during project execution. When others don't hear updates, their understanding of your project becomes a fog. "No news is good news" is not the best form of communication inside a product development organization. Instead, you should provide clarity so your partners know whether the product delivery is expected to be on time, or whether they need to adjust their own schedules to accommodate delays. Send a regular status update, ideally in tandem with your process for updating your project plan.

Artifacts

Status updates

A status update should be at the right level of detail for the audience. Sharing the entire project plan is not useful because it's too detailed. The art is in finding the right granularity that breaks the work into understandable milestones or independently running tracks. These milestones or tracks should be easily understood by the audience. Each can be described as being *on track*, *at risk*, or *blocked*. If at risk, list the risks – perhaps someone reading the status update can provide some help to de-risk that track. If blocked, list the reason why. Again, your audience of sponsors and stakeholders may be able to help.

Validation

Throughout execution, you'll be validating that the under-development product is moving closer toward the final working product. You'll use the internal team to do this validation via *Dogfooding, QA Testing, and User Acceptance Testing*.

Dogfooding

Dogfooding refers to when employees use the product in their day-to-day activities. Employees can be a good source of feedback and bug reports. But dogfooding works best when the product is something the employees of the company can actually use in their day-to-day lives.

QA Testing

The QA team will run through its QA test procedures, ensuring all the behavior defined in the PRD has been tested on all supported platforms. In addition to testing the expected behavior, the QA team also tests for unexpected outcomes by attempting to do the opposite of what you would expect a normal user to do. For example, the QA team will try unsupported inputs to make sure they are properly rejected, will wait for timeouts, and so forth.

User Acceptance Testing (UAT)

User Acceptance Testing is meant to be done by "users", but in reality this means someone who can speak for users, such as the product manager, a UX team member; or, in the case of enterprise/internal software, someone who will actually use the software. Whereas the QA team has been performing testing based off of a spec, in UAT the tester is expected to actually understand how the product is intended to be used and how it fits into a workflow. UAT should be done in as close to the actual environment as possible to run the product through its paces.

Phase 5: Launch

Cheat sheet: Launch

Purpose

The Launch phase is when you actually release the product to the world. This is the exciting moment the team has been working toward.

Partners
    Eng team, XFN partners such as customer support, marketing, PR

Activities
    Closing out all remaining issues, getting approvals to launch, putting plans into action

Artifacts
    Marketing plan, by the Marketing team
    Public relations plan, by the PR team
    Support scripts, by the Support team
    Metrics dashboards, by the Data Science team or engineering team
    Monitoring dashboards, by the engineering team
    Validation
    Market response, by the Marketing team
    KPIs, by the PM, engineering team, or data science team
    Monitoring, by the engineering team

Purpose

The Launch phase is when you actually release the product to the world. This is the exciting moment the team has been working toward.

Partners

Eng team, XFN partners such as customer support, marketing, and PR

Activities

There is a lot of work that goes into ensuring a smooth launch. The product manager engages the entire cross-functional team ahead of the launch to do this. The following questions need to be answered in advance, and should be answered in documents written by a cross functional partner:

- Where and how will we reach our target audience? How is the product positioned and what is our message?
- What is the likely press reaction, and what will our response be to inquiries?
- What issues are customers most likely to encounter, and how can we guide them to solutions?
- How will we measure success?
- How can we be sure everything is working properly?
- Do we have all the required approvals?

The product manager can help ensure the best outcome for each of these plans by bringing together the right groups of team members to review the plans.

Final approvals

The approvals plan first mentioned in the *Planning* stage should be reviewed before launch. Whereas in that earlier phase, there may have been provisional approvals based on the plan, now each approver should re-approve based on the actual completed product. Getting explicit approval ensures that key partners and governance teams have had an opportunity to flag any problems or risks before the launch is live.

Team readiness

The working group should review the final product and launch plan with sponsors and team leaders to confirm their plan is complete and they have approval from their leadership to launch.

Launch day

Launching usually involves a lot more than just pushing a single button. There are often dozens of processes to kick off and verify. Setting up a detailed list of what needs to be done and by whom helps to ensure nothing gets missed. For a big launch, getting everyone together to complete the launch activities from start-to-finish helps ensure key people can be reached in the event of a problem during launch. It's also an exhilarating team bonding experience to watch a product go live together..

Artifacts

Marketing Plan

The Marketing plan will outline the communications aspects of the Go To Market strategy. Who are the target customers and where are they found? What are the distribution channels that will be releasing the product? Where will the product be announced, and by whom? What is the advertising budget? In what channels and what markets will ads run?

An outline of the messages that will be delivered in each channel can be found in this document. As the team gets closer to launch, drafts of what the actual copy will be are found here.

You'll work with your marketing team on the Go To Market plan.

Public Relations plan

Everyone wants happy customers, an accepting marketplace and positive press reviews. Being fully prepared requires taking the contrarian view: what are all the things that could go wrong? Who is going to be pissed off that you launched your product? What are the government, competitive, or consumer complaints that you're likely to receive?

There are probably a million ways that your launch can go wrong, and it may not be possible to head off every risk before launch. What you can do, however, is write up a list of potential problems that may come up and how you would respond to them. Often in the process of enumerating risks and responses, you will find risk-mitigating changes you can make before you launch.

If your organization has a PR person, work with them to play out all the possible negative reactions the press or public might have, and how you'll handle them.

If it makes sense, you may reach out to the press ahead of time to secure written stories about your launch. News organizations are in the business of publishing stories, and if yours is interesting, they'll typically cover your product on launch day. By sharing details of your product ahead of time and "under embargo", you give the press time to ask you clarifying questions and get a story put together so it can run the same day as your product launch.

Articles written about you are known as *earned advertising*. Because it's news, not an advertisement, you don't pay for it.

Support Plan

What are all the touchpoints needed to ensure customers can access and achieve success with the product? For example, where do customers go when they have questions or problems? Is help built into the product? Are there message boards or dedicated support channels? What kind of documentation is provided? If new features are being released for an existing product, are customer support agents aware of the feature ahead of time and have they been trained on how to talk to customers about it? Have you defined appeasement or refund policies for unhappy customers?

The support team should write the support plan, but the product and engineering team should review it to be sure it's providing accurate directions.

Measurement and Metrics Plan

To land well you also need to know how customers are using your product. Not only how many customers, but how successful they are in your product. Are the key user journeys being completed with the expected success rate? Or are users abandoning the journeys early? Where are the users coming from? How often do they use your product, etc.

You'll work with the Data Science team on the metrics plan. To measure, the product needs to be properly instrumented for the start, including tracking clickstreams and tracking any funnel conversion points. This work needs to have been thought through early on during the Definition stage.

Monitoring Plan

While *metrics* are about user behavior, *monitoring* is about system health. Establish monitoring to be sure you know when a component of your system is failing. Users don't have patience for crashing apps or websites that are down. Monitoring is the job of the eng or "eng prod" (production engineering) team. As the product manager, you want to ensure they've thought this through and set everything up.

And always remember: even if system health is being measured, if the system isn't set up to alert someone on the team when there are problems at 3am, it won't be of any help.

Dashboards

If metrics and monitoring data is hard to access, it won't be looked at. Setting up dashboards that are accessible by everyone working on the launch – not only the engineers who set them up – ensures that the metrics can be looked at constantly after the launch happens.

Validation

Smoke test

The key validation of a launch is the *smoke test*, a run through of the critical user journeys in the production environment.

Crash counts

Ideally your product is instrumented so software crashes are automatically logged into a tracking system. Keeping an eye on crash counts in the hours after a launch will help uncover any bugs or release-related problems that weren't caught in QA or during the smoke test.

Phase 6: Land

Cheat sheet: Land

Purpose

Launching is getting the product out. Landing is ensuring that users are getting what they expected out of the product and it's gaining the expected traction.

Partners

Marketing, Customer support, Engineering

Activities

A/B tests, fast follows and bug fixes

Artifacts

Press feedback, by the PR team
Customer support inquiries, by the Support team

Validation

Metrics, by the PM or data science team
Growth, by the data science or business team
Life Time Value (LTV), by the business team

Purpose

Landing is ensuring that users are getting what they expected out of the product and it's gaining the expected traction. You can't turn your back after the launch. There are various ways to measure the uptake of the product after launch.

Partners

Marketing, Customer support, Engineering

Activities

Customer support reviews

Customers who are having issues with your product will reach out to your support channels. Make sure you have a very open line of communication with support so you understand what kinds of issues users are having.

Sometimes the lines of communication between support channels and the product team are totally broken. In the case of outsourced support, where success is measured by the percent of cases closed and the speed with which issues are resolved, you'll often get a false signal. Customer issues may get resolved quickly without actually solving the customer's problem. I've been contacted directly by frustrated users who've found me on LinkedIn when they've been unable to make any headway with official product support channels.

You may want to test your product support channel yourself

or listen in on live or recorded calls to get a sense of the actual problems users are having with your product and what the support experience is like.

A/B tests

A/B tests can help to test hypotheses the team had before launch, but which couldn't be proven or disproven with UXR testing. For example, parameters can be tuned and multiple variations of the UI can be tested. A/B tests provide a quantitative approach to getting data about how users react to your product at scale.

Fast follows and bug fixes

If your launch was date driven and you launched with a reduced feature set in order to get the product out the door on schedule, launching "fast follows" means releasing minor updates that add features that weren't completed in time for the initial launch. Fast follows may also contain fixes to bugs that were known at the time of launch, but were not launch blocking. Bugs that are discovered post launch may be fixed as fast follows if they're discovered right away; otherwise they become part of regular maintenance, described next.

Artifacts

Press feedback

Ideally you've made some buzz with your product launch and have generated some press. Collecting feedback from the press, blogs, Reddit, Twitter, etc give you insight into how your product is being received.

Validation

Product success begins with a bold vision or an insightful idea. But ultimately real users are the arbiters of whether your product fits into their life or not. Achieving product market fit is a continuous process that kicks into high gear once your product is out in the marketplace. Finding product market fit involves identifying the right audience, reaching them, convincing them to try the product, and ultimately retaining them as users. If you don't have the expected traction right away, it's up to you to identify the gap between the product and customer expectations. And working with the marketing team, ensuring your product is being placed in front of the target audience in the places they expect to find it.

Phase 7: Maintain

Cheat sheet: Maintain

Purpose
   The maintenance phase involves ensuring the product continues to serve the target users, fixing top users

issues, and keeping the product current amid changing infrastructure technologies.

Partners
   Eng team, Customer support team

Activities
   Bug triage, Engineering maintenance and migrations, Deprecation

Purpose

The maintenance phase involves ensuring the product continues to serve the target users, fixing top users issues, and keeping the product current amid changing infrastructure technologies.

Partners

Eng team, Customer support team

Activities

Customer Support Reviews

Customer support reviews should continue during the maintenance phase. Even though your product may not have changed, customer support requests can uncover incompatibilities with new software or new usage patterns. Plus, it's likely you're still releasing updates to the product, which may trigger new issues.

Bug triage

Despite the team's best efforts, your product is going to have issues that cause users pain. The issues may be software bugs – i.e., software coding errors that cause an application to crash. The issues may be more subtle, like a failure to properly handle an edge case that wasn't thought of during product development. The product may also be hard or confusing to use, causing challenges for users who can't figure out how to do the things they're supposed to be able to do.

You'll need to develop a process to ensure issues get triaged for impact and severity and are prioritized appropriately for fixing. I'll go into greater detail on setting up a bug triaging process in the Process section later in this book.

Engineering maintenance and migrations

The world never stands still. It's unlikely that your product is fully independent from other systems. Often when those systems – be it databases, web services, or other – undergo major updates, you need to update your product to stay current. The engineering team should stay abreast of these requirements and allocate time to maintain the software and migrate off older dependencies.

4

Validation

"If I had asked people what they wanted, they would have said faster horses."
–*Henry Ford*

Throughout the product development life cycle, you should continuously validate your ideas through some objective litmus tests to be sure you're investing the team's time and energies in the right direction. Validation gives you something to point to that makes the team comfortable that your ideas are rooted in solid ground. The further along you get toward launching your product, the more concrete the testing should become.

Once your vision clicks for you, it will seem painfully obvious, perhaps even inevitable. Once you have an insight, you'll see it as plainly as if it has already become reality. If only you could just speed things up and get it developed and launched! But remember that others have not yet seen the outcome in their mind's eye. They may not agree that what you want to do is possible, or they may not agree that it's as valuable to customers as you think and therefore not worthwhile. You may also be wrong.

Don't get impatient; instead: test, validate and be grateful to your critics. They can point out something you've missed in your thinking. It's not enough to provide an inspiring vision, it's also your job to provide the validating information that gets everyone on the team comfortable with that vision.

Let me give you two examples of when my team or I myself have been wrong, and validation helped avoid a bad outcome.

The first example is about the marketing proposition for a VPN. A former team developed a VPN that had some pretty cool networking properties. In addition to protecting user privacy, as most VPNs do, this VPN improved network reliability by doing behind-the-scenes magic. The engineers who were responsible for improving networking performance believed that users would love the idea of using a VPN to get better networking. Because the team built it, and because they thought it was useful, they assumed everyone else would love it, too.

However, when the team market tested the value proposition based around network performance, users were skeptical. First, everyday users were unable to grok a value proposition about networking improvements. The message was simplified, but that didn't help, because networking is just about the most opaque topic there is. Second, users had heard negative news about VPNs: word on the street was that VPNs could siphon all your traffic and mine it for data. The bottom line was that users were extremely suspicious of being offered a VPN that could steal their data while being told a story about networking performance. It felt like a bait-and-switch.

The team did further research to understand users' basic needs and learned that users didn't believe they were encountering networking issues at all. It made no difference that the team could measure that they were! However, users were very concerned about maintaining their privacy. When we released our VPN, we touted its privacy features as the primary benefit, knowing that was the message that resonated best with users.

The second example comes from this book that you're reading right now. The working title for this book was *Rockstar Product Management*. In tech, it's great to be called a rockstar, so I assumed *Rockstar Product Management* would be a desirable title to most readers interested in the role. What do you think of that title?

I market tested the title via a survey. I asked people to rate the likelihood that they would buy various books on product management based on the title. Of the ten titles tested in the survey, *Rockstar Product Management* came in dead last.

In both of these cases, the customer and the product team did not have the same expectations. When developing a product, it's easy to get wrapped up in what you're creating. What you're doing can start to take on importance simply because you're doing it. That's why it's so critical to check in and validate with real users at key points throughout the product development process.

Excitement about an idea is not a substitute for validation. Even if you're right, if you're lacking credible reasoning and evidence upon which your product vision rests, you will undoubtedly face detractors whose skepticism may hinder your progress in the organization. Those who have vision succeed at validation are called visionary; those who provide vision but no support are called crazy. Often what is needed to bridge the gap is evidence.

Before we get too far, let me address the contrarian view. Steve Jobs said, "It's really hard to design products by focus groups. A lot of times, people don't know what they want until you show it to them." I have seen leaders of companies invoke this mantra to an extreme, perform zero market validation, and then fail. While Jobs may be right that you can't count on focus groups to design your final product or solution for you, customers are still the best source for information about customer needs.

A focus group of customers off the street is unlikely to have designed the iPod. But Jobs saw what customers were *doing* – they were listening to music on portable tape and CD players, which required carrying around tapes and CDs. Jobs saw a big opportunity there. Lots of people were already listening to music on the go, but it was a high friction activity to carry all that bulky media. Understanding the market size for portable music players helps ensure the problem was worth solving. If Apple could make a beautiful, easy-to-use alternative to clunky tape and CD players, it could be reasonably certain it would capture a good share of the portable player market and even expand that market. The key was understanding the user problem – listening to music on the go – and validating the market opportunity.

Remember Henry Ford? He said, "If I had asked people what they wanted, they would have said faster horses." Validation is not asking your customers to invent the next automobile. Validation means making sure your product is solving an actual problem people have, and that it's worthwhile for you to solve it. It doesn't mean asking your customers to design your product, but does mean ensuring that the problems they have are solved by the solution you intend to deliver.

A challenge for early electric cars was that their range was abysmal. Very few people bought them as a result. Yes, Teslas were beautiful, but what really set them apart was long range batteries that had comparable range to a tank of gas. Tesla didn't need testers to drive its cars for months to determine the optimal battery charge. It's intuitive that customers need to have a single charge last at least as long as that of the car they were replacing. By accounting for that basic need, Musk propelled Tesla's market cap to be larger than all other car companies combined.

Validation does not occur at a single point in time. You will need to validate your product all along the journey from idea inception to after you launch. But you will validate in different ways during different stages of the product life cycle:

1. Early on, when you only have an idea – or perhaps you don't even have an idea yet, but only a direction or a "space" you want to explore – **market research** can help you understand existing offerings and user needs.
2. When you have a rough idea of what shape your product might take, and you have designs that can be put in front of real people, **usability testing** can help gauge the response to that product's form factor, user interface, and capabilities.
3. When your product is in development, you, your team, and beta testers can put the product through its paces to ensure it delivers on its promise with **dogfood testing**.
4. And after you release your product, you'll improve its market fit with constant tweaking via **A/B testing**.

I'll go into each of these types of validation in more detail below. Before we jump in, let's build up some definitions for how we talk about users.

Talking about users

When we talk about users, there are different ways to divide them up. Four common terms you'll hear are segments, personas, and cohorts, and slices. You should know how these differ, and when to use each term.

Market segments

Segmentation is most often synonymous with *market* segmentation, and the terms *segment, market,* and *market segment* are often used interchangeably.

In *Crossing the Chasm,* Jeffrey Moore defines a market as "a set of actual or potential customers for a given set of products or services, who have a common set of needs or wants, and who reference each other when making a buying decision."

By "reference each other," Moore asks, would they find each other at a trade conference? These days, you might also consider a trade conference to be virtual, like a Reddit forum. A difference in language, geography or industry could prevent two potential customers from being in the same segment because they'd never talk to each other. Even though a chef and a moving company both buy digital scales, they are not in the same market segment, because they'd rarely speak to one another when making a purchasing decision. It turns out they also have very different needs when it comes to scales.

An interior designer in the United States and an interior designer in China would also be in different market segments, because they'd never communicate with each other when making purchasing decisions. The styles their customers are interested in may also differ substantially.

Defining your target market up-front is important to do to be sure there is in fact an audience for your product. You should decide whether you'll target consumers or enterprise customers. Which countries or regions will you target? Which industry vertical will you start with? E.g., insurance companies in the U.S., lawyers in France, or athletes in English-speaking countries.

Defining segments is critical during the earliest stages of

product development when the opportunity itself is being validated.

Personas

Personas help the team form an intuition for the users in their target market. Personas are created for each user type. Personas bring the user types to life by giving them names and describing the types of challenges they have. They paint a picture that helps the team develop empathy. For example, think of Roda the Runner, Sally the Subway Rider, and Cathy the Classical Music Enthusiast. When designing a hypothetical music player interface, each of these users will have distinct needs.

Personas are helpful any time distinct user types have distinct needs. For example, a parent and child user might require distinct persona definitions to reflect different expectations when using the product. In a collaborative enterprise product or a consumer product sold as a family plan, a group member and a group administrator will require different features based on their relationship to the group.

Defining personas helps to ensure your product definition is complete. Do they need any distinct capabilities? For any given capability, how should it work for each persona? Are there any workflows or interactions between personas?

A common mistake is to create lots of personas that differ in subtle ways that may not be relevant to the product definition. For example, if the distinction between multiple personas is their age, but there's no difference in their needs, there's no need for separate personas.

Personas are used during product definition and development.

Cohorts

Cohorts are samples of users from the same segment, typically used for analysis by direct comparison. For example, when you launch a product change to improve user engagement, you should run an A/B test to validate your hypothesis. To do so, you create *cohorts*, which are groups of users randomly selected from a larger group. One cohort is always the *control* group; this group continues to receive the current product experience. Other cohorts are experiment groups; they see the new experience, potentially with multiple variations. By simultaneously showing different experiences to different cohorts, you can determine which experience performs best. I'll discuss A/B testing in detail later in this chapter.

Slices

You may want to analyze existing product features based on some property of your users. For example: tenure, number of purchases, geography, hardware used to access your service, or some combination. Do new and tenured users respond to promotions differently? Are users who have already made purchases early in their tenure more likely to make another purchase later in their tenure?

Whereas cohorts are used to sort users into different experiences, slices are used post-facto for analysis of different users who saw the same experience.

As a review:

- User segments are used during the product opportunity definition and market validation
- Personas are used during product definition and development
- Cohorts are used for creating A/B test experiment groups
- Slices are used to segment users during post-facto analysis

Types of research

Market research

A product manager needs to understand the market as deeply as possible. They should know who the other players are and what offerings are in the market already. They should also understand customers in the market and their needs. By understanding both sides, the team can identify areas where existing products and solutions don't satisfy customer needs. These "white spaces" where no current solutions exist are opportunities where the team can innovate and provide solutions.

First pass market research can be done yourself, through direct research of existing products and solutions by examining the market offering by offering.

You can also find existing market research. Many companies'

sole purpose is to do market research and publish prepackaged information. For example, Gartner and Statista are great starting points.

Often the marketing team or business strategy team in your company can help you identify existing market research, or initiate research on your behalf.

User needs research

It's tempting to think we have all the answers, but we have to remind ourselves that we are not the customer. Direct communication with potential customers will help you better understand their needs. Depending on the type of information you're looking for, either the marketing team or the UXR team can help with this type of research.

User needs research can be done through interviews or surveys. Interviews tend toward a type of research known as "qualitative", because questions have open-ended answers, and responses must be interpreted. Surveys tend toward "quantitative" research, because questions tend to have a limited set of potential answers and the results are more amenable to aggregation and computation. I'll go into each of these types of research in detail.

Quantitative research

If your product is going to solve a specific problem that you think a lot of people have, ask them. Quantitative surveys of large numbers of users can help validate that you're in the right ballpark. You might be surprised to find that people either don't have the problem you thought they had, or that they don't feel as strongly as you that it's a problem worth solving. A method that works well is to define a problem scenario and ask users two questions:

1. How often do you experience this problem?
2. How important is it for you that this problem gets solved?

You can plot the responses on a 2x2 graph to see what resonates with potential customers.

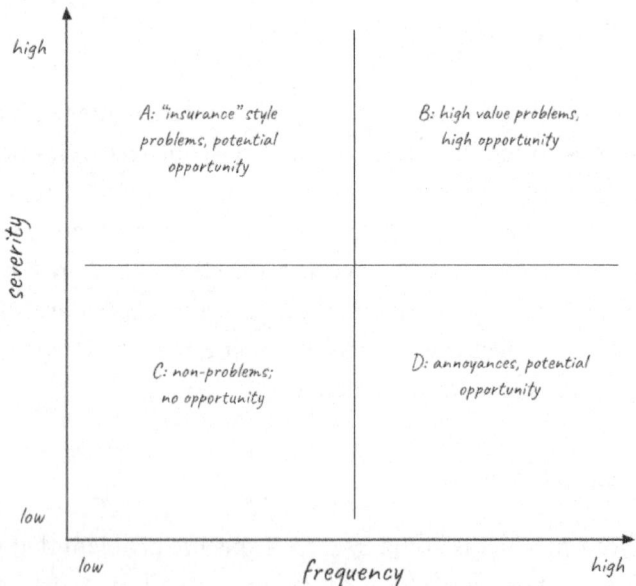

high

A: "insurance" style problems, potential opportunity

B: high value problems, high opportunity

severity

C: non-problems; no opportunity

D: annoyances, potential opportunity

low

low   frequency   high

Quadrant B represents problems that are high frequency and high severity. These are good problems to solve. Users will derive a lot of value from your solution, and there will be plenty of opportunities to charge customers for it.

Quadrant D represents problems that are high frequency but low severity. These problems also present an opportunity. While the problem may not be severe, it is annoying. So long as the solution is easy enough to implement and it comes at the right price, users may be motivated to buy it.

Quadrant A represents problems that are high severity and low frequency. These are trickier. Clearly users need the service, because the problems are high severity. However, because they encounter the problem infrequently, they are unlikely to become loyal repeat customers. Problems of this type often fall into "insurance" categories. If you get into a bad car accident, the bills to repair your car and your medical bills may be astronomically high. No one is prepared to pay for those surprise expenses when they happen. Yet no one wants to pay for insurance, either, because 99.9% of the time they don't need it. This is why most insurance coverage is mandated; if it wasn't, most people wouldn't buy it.

Quadrant C, infrequently occurring, low-severity issues, are not worth solving at all.

When designing a survey, in addition to asking the two magic questions, you should also ask qualifying questions that screen to ensure the person is actually in the target market segment. You can also ask any other questions that will let you slice up the results in useful ways for additional analysis. These sorts of questions will vary from case to case, and might include whether the respondents use any similar or complementary services to your own, how much they pay for similar services, etc.

Although the tools are always changing, Google Surveys, Mechanical Turk, and Qualtrics are good starting points. Your company may have its own preferred tools for this kind of research, or you can easily research online what is the latest and greatest.

Qualitative research

Qualitative research consists of open-ended questions. These questions are valuable as they can provide insights you wouldn't normally get from quantitative surveys. In a quantitative survey, users select from predefined answers. In qualitative research, you can hear how people actually think, and may get answers you hadn't even thought of. Hearing how actual customers see the world and understand information and tools can be very eye-opening.

Finding appropriate people to interview can be a challenge if you don't have the support of a big organization that's used to running research. Conducting qualitative research one subject at a time can also be very time consuming and costly. Analysis of all the data is another time consuming, painstaking step.

Common pitfalls

As useful as surveys and interviews are, they also suffer from some pitfalls.

Study participants are only human: they want to be right and they want to please the study facilitator. Both of these desires can lead you to invalid results. There's a danger that you may tip the participants off to the "right answer" that you're looking for. An experienced researcher will structure the survey and questions to elicit actual data that provides the team with insights rather than lead the participants to provide desirable answers that make the team feel good.

Another danger is that what users *report* they would do in a scenario is often not the same as what they actually *will* do in that scenario. It's not that they are lying. People typically act unconsciously, based on reflex. When in a simulated environment, study subjects may not actually be able to accurately report what they would do in the real world, because their conscious mind is involved during the study, and it isn't involved in the actual moment where the choice occurs. The result is that study participants often report what they *aspire* to do. A solution to this problem is to ask the study participant to identify the last time a specific situation occurred. Then ask them concrete questions about what they actually did then rather than ask them what they hypothetically might do in a similar future situation.

Another danger of any user research is the potential to draw conclusions from small numbers of participants, or "*small*

N counts". For a quantitative consumer survey launched on Mechanical Turk, you may be able to gather thousands of responses quickly, limited only by your budget, and feel relatively confident in the aggregated results. However, a qualitative study based on interviews may take at least an hour per participant to administer. Studies like these are often capped at 10 participants. With such small numbers, only a few outlier participants can throw the result off.

Finally, beware of looking to averages instead of looking at all the data, and understanding its shape. The following three data sets – A, B, and C – all have the same average, but they represent very different distributions. In A, users are evenly distributed across high, medium and low. In B, all users are middle-of-the-road. In C, users cluster in high or low.

Averages can be deceiving

Expert researchers are trained in all of these areas, but because of these dangers, the product manager should stay involved in the structuring of survey and study questions to be sure she can rely on the results. She should verify that the study provides an opportunity to gather data on all key questions, and also to verify that there are no leading questions. Even then, user needs studies should always be viewed with a grain of salt – as a data point and not a conclusion.

Types of user testing

Usability testing

When the solution you intend to bring to market is novel, usability research, undertaken by the User Experience Research (UXR) team, can be invaluable to ensure users understand the product interface.

Usability studies can be undertaken early, at the stage when mocks of the product interface are available, and before actual implementation work has begun.

Using early prototypes of the product – "paper prototypes", mocks shown in sequence, or clickable mock-based prototypes – the UX researcher walks potential users through scenarios to see if and how they would use the product to get through the scenarios.

These step-by-step walkthroughs can give insight into whether the user would actually employ the product to solve their problems. Can the user tell, based on how the product is positioned, that the product will solve the intended problem? Or do they misunderstand the intent of the product entirely, and are unable to connect the stated problem with the interface you've presented them with? Then, is the user able to successfully and easily get the job done, or is the interface confusing, cumbersome, and opaque, causing them to fail?

In usability research, users should never be made to feel bad for not being able to complete tasks with your interface. On the contrary, when you learn through usability testing that users can't figure out your product *before you've actually built it*, you've dodged a huge bullet. Relish all the ways users can't figure out your product because they are opportunities to improve your interface before spending actual time and money building it.

Dogfooding

Validation continues after you've started development. When you experience bugs in your product *yourself*, and when you get stuck in stilted user experiences *yourself*, you suddenly have a real appreciation for how the user is experiencing your product. To truly have empathy for your users and their needs, you've got to get into their shoes.

Product teams should "eat their own dogfood". This means that they should make using their product part of their day-to-day lives whenever possible. The saying originates from actual dog food: if the product is good enough for the people who designed the dog food to eat it, then it must be good enough for the actual dogs, too.

If you only test your product just before launch, you'll only be checking your original assumptions about how the product should work. But you won't experience how the product actually works, situationally. In real life, your needs as a real user may be very different than when you're testing planned scenarios in a controlled environment. When the use case for your product comes up in real life, do you naturally reach for it? Does it fit the situation in the way you expected? Does it solve the problem?

Ideally you will continue to use your product after launch, too. If you don't use your own product, it's easy to become numb to issues reported through customer support channels. Users can quickly be viewed as complainers. Especially when they're aggrieved and vitriolic, it can be hard to sympathize.

If your team doesn't fit into the target audience of the product, set up "dogfood days" where the team gets together to work through scenarios using the product to find bugs and experience the user journeys first hand. These sessions are invaluable to give the team first hand experience and build user empathy.

A/B Testing

What is it?

A/B testing is a scientifically and statistically sound method of determining how changes in your product affect outcomes. A/B testing is most relevant when making changes to an existing product. For example, when you release an update, you want to know that what you've released is better than what was there before. Rather than closing your eyes and hoping for the best, A/B testing can validate that the new version is actually better.

A/B testing derives its name from two groups, group A and group B, each of which sees a different version of your product. One group is always a control group and sees the existing product experience. One or more experiment groups see variations. By observing how the users in each group behave, you can determine which variation performs best.

When to use A/B testing

Use A/B testing when rolling out new features, to test multiple options for a feature, or to tune parameters. You can use an A/B experiment to compare interface flows – for example, to optimize a sales funnel. Shockingly, minor changes to fonts, sizes, colors, and placement can make big differences to user buying behavior. Amazon was an early pioneer in this type of experimentation, running hundreds if not thousands of experiments on buy buttons and checkout flows. The results were not always beautiful, but they improved conversion. Whenever transactions are at play, you should always make changes as experiments. It would be gut wrenching to launch a beautiful new design that results in lost revenues due to the introduction of an extra click, or a button that became harder to locate. An A/B test would quantitatively reveal the new design's deficiencies so they could be addressed before a full launch.

A/B testing can also be used to seek out optimal parameters.

For example, let's say you're the product manager for an online blackjack game. Your goal is to have players play for as long as possible, while also losing money over the long term. You have a hypothesis that getting dealt a blackjack increases the length of a session, but too many blackjacks cost the casino its profits. You can set up multiple experiment arms, each set to a different probability of a given hand resulting in a blackjack. Over a sufficiently long period of time, you can correlate the average session length in each group and the profitability of those sessions with the parameters. (Note that this is just a step or two away from becoming a machine learning model.)

The same mechanism used to run an A/B experiment can be used when rolling out new features to ensure the rollout is working as expected. When using A/B testing to test the impact of a new feature, the feature should be launched in an off state, controlled by A/B testing parameters. The control group sees the existing software, and the experiment group sees the new features. You can first ramp up the experiment group to 1% to ensure there are no errors or unexpected problems with the launch. Then ramp up to 10%, and then 50%. At 50%, you can compare how the control and experiment groups behave. When satisfied that the new feature is behaving as expected, you can move to 100% and fully launch the feature. Product managers should be in sync with their engineering team on rollout schedules following this pattern and monitor metrics closely throughout.

How to do it

A/B testing involves assigning users randomly to a control group and to one or more experiment groups.

The experiment groups should be designed with care. Observe the scientific method and change only one variable at a time. If you have multiple variables to test, have enough groups so you can see the independent effects as well as the combined effects of each variable.

For example, the following grouping is OK because the variables x and y can be assessed independently or together:

- Control group: $x = 1, y = 1$
- Experiment Group A: $x = 2, y = 1$
- Experiment Group B: $x = 1, y = 2$
- Experiment Group C: $x = 2, y = 2$

When running an A/B test, you should know what you're trying to optimize and be sure you can measure it. For example, clicks, sales, basket size, session length, etc.

Common validity pitfalls

A/B testing relies on the scientific method, allowing you to observe how individual changes to your product result in different outcomes between a control group and an experiment group.

To be sure you don't derive false conclusions from your

experiments, pay attention to the following common pitfalls.

Statistical significance

How do you know your results are not just based on random chance? Are some outlier users skewing the results for the winning group? The more data you have, the more confident you can be in the result. To gather more data, you either need more users in each group, or more time. But how many users and how much time is enough?

When you've gathered enough data, your experiment is said to have achieved "statistical significance". There are mathematical formulas to estimate many data points you'll need to achieve statistical significance, but they're beyond the scope of this book. This is where data scientists shine. Once you've achieved statistical significance, the results can be trusted. Before that point, you would be unwise to draw conclusions from the data, as tempting as it may be to do so.

Another method to estimate when an experiment has reached statistical significance – or to expose when data has gone askew – is to establish multiple groups with the exact same experimental definition. For example, two control groups or two identical experiment groups. The behavior of the identical groups is expected to converge. If the identical groups don't exhibit the same behavior, you either don't have statistical significance, or there is some flaw in the experiment setup.

Unlike groups

Be sure that your experiment groups are randomly assigned from the same set of users. If users in the experiment group and control group are unlike one another, then the experiment will not be valid. For example, if the control group is all tenured users and the experiment group is all new users, you will not get a valid result.

To understand how different groups respond to the same experience, instead of an A/B test, work with your data science team to slice up your metrics based on user profile data. This analysis doesn't require an A/B test, but simply post-facto analysis of regular usage. To do such an analysis, you'll need a way to identify user attributes that define the slices in your data logs that can be used in the analysis.

Changes mid-experiment

Making changes mid-experiment invalidates the experiment. Whether changing group composition or changing the treatments shown to each group during the experiment, experiment data can't be trusted once a change has been made. If you find a bug, of course fix it, but know that you will have to restart the experiment.

Comparing different time periods

It's tempting to test treatments sequentially – say one per week – and compare the results after all the experimental treatments have been tested. While this is indeed tempting, this approach does not produce valid results.

Let's say you have a few treatments of a buy button. One was used during a Halloween sale, and another was used during Black Friday, and the third was used in January. Can you deduce anything about buying behavior based on the differences in the site treatments? Unfortunately not. The seasonality and presence or absence of holidays is going to be a larger contributing factor to changes in user behavior than variations in your buy button.

The only valid way to test the three treatments is to split up the same group of shoppers into randomized A/B test cohorts and show each group a different treatment during the same time period, and compare those results.

Product-market fit

New products begin with a bold vision or an insightful idea. All of the validation techniques mentioned in this chapter help you de-risk your product launch. But ultimately real users are the arbiters of whether your product fits into their lives or not. Finding product-market fit involves identifying the right audience, reaching them, convincing them to try the product, and ultimately retaining them as users. The quality of the product solution and its implementation, which has been the subject of this chapter, is but one element.

Achieving product-market fit is a continuous process that stays in high gear even after your product is out in the marketplace.

5

Tools of the Trade

This section provides templates that you'll use on a regular basis in your job as a product manager. I'll go into a lot of detail in each of these in this chapter. Here is a quick description of what's to come.

First, I'll introduce a *Two Pager* and *Vision Deck*. A two-pager or vision deck is useful to explain a product direction at a conceptual level without getting into all the nitty gritty. These two contain essentially the same content but in different presentation formats – text document or presentation deck – and are used at slightly different stages at the project. These materials help you get buy-in for your project.

Next I'll dive into the *Product Requirements Document*, or PRD. The PRD is the key artifact the PM will create during the product development process that aligns the whole team on what is to be built by the engineering team. It serves as a complete specification of the product deliverable, and every other function – e.g., QA, customer support, legal – can look to it for clarity on how the product will behave.

I'll then talk through a *Project plan*. There are a zillion tools on the market for project management. Whether you choose to use online planning software, or just create a simple spreadsheet yourself to track the team's work, you'll benefit from having a solid understanding of what should be included in a project plan. You'll learn everything you need to know here.

I'll then walk you through building a *Roadmap*. The roadmap is a high level timeline; it may describe a single project, in which case it's a zoomed out version of your project plan. More likely, a roadmap zooms out even further and describes how a series of projects fit together over a longer period to achieve a bigger vision. The roadmap starts with where you are now and it ends with your larger vision being realized.

Finally I'll talk through some day-to-day tips for running meetings – an indispensable skill for product managers who are often in meetings all day. I'll conclude this section with an example of a meeting agenda to help set structure for your meetings.

Now, let's dive in.

Two-pager / Vision deck

A two-pager or vision deck is useful to explain a product direction at a conceptual level without getting into all the nitty gritty that is required in a PRD. These documents are key communication drivers to help you secure stakeholder buy-in. They often contain roughly the same information. The text version of the document is most useful as a working document within the team coming up with the idea. Once the idea is firmed up, recasting the information in a presentation format that allows for walking stakeholders and executive sponsors through the idea at a high level.

The key sections you'll want in your two pager are the following. You may of course add other content, but these are essential:

1. Problem statement
2. Opportunity
3. Strategy
4. Visualization / Mocks
5. Objectives & Key Results
6. Key metrics
7. Validation
8. Milestones
9. Risks

I'll go into more detail on each of these sections below.

Problem statement

What is the current state and how is it problematic? What goal are users trying to accomplish that they can't easily achieve today?

Opportunity

What outcome can be expected by solving this problem? A market-sizing is often helpful here to put the opportunity in context. Is it a big problem for a large class of people? How many potential users are there, and how much potential revenue is at stake?

Strategy

How will your product reach your users (i.e., distribution channels or partners)? Is there a business model innovation at play? Anything that speaks to how you'll seize upon the opportunity goes here.

Visualization / Mocks

As they say, a picture tells a thousand words. Nothing gets the point across like concrete visuals of what a product experience will look like. At this early stage of a 2-pager or vision deck, visualizations can be highly conceptual. It's most important to give the audience an understanding of where and how the product makes contact with the end-user. Identifying and showcasing the top one or two critical user journeys (CUJs) is ideal. Getting too detailed by showing each product screen is likely to be counterproductive as it invites feedback on the specific design rather than the high level concept.

Objectives & Key Results

Objectives are concrete deliverables that need to be delivered to fulfill the strategy. Writing objectives along with "key results" ensures your objectives are measurable. For example,

Objective: Worldwide distribution network secured
   Key result 1: North America partner signed by end of Q2
   Key result 2: EMEA partner signed by end of Q3
   Key result 3: LATAM partner signed by end of Q4

Key metrics

How will you measure success? This might be monthly or daily active users, sales, profit, etc.

Validation

What are the early validation points where you'll confirm that the project has product market fit and is gaining traction? These may be user studies, market research, pre-orders, etc. See also the complete section on Validation in this book.

Milestones

Give a sense of time to your project with key milestones. When will the objectives – or key dependencies to achieve them – be delivered? If there are any external dates that drive the timeline, e.g., Black Friday, tie them in here. Not quite a full product roadmap, this section highlights the most interesting outcomes from a stakeholder/sponsor's perspective.

Risks

What are the reasons why this plan may not succeed? Risks may come from competition, regulation, or internal execution risk, e.g, lack of appropriate resources within your company. Identifying the risks up-front helps to align stakeholders on how to de-risk the project. For example, if you know you don't have appropriate resources within the company, part of the plan may be to hire consultants.

Product Requirements Document (PRD)

The Product Requirements Document, commonly referred to as a PRD, is the key artifact the PM will create during the product development process that aligns the whole team on what is to be built. Writing this document is a lot of work, but once the PRD is written, agreed upon, and approved, the PM can likely go on holiday for a month or two and no one will notice (just kidding).

The PRD is a clarifying document and should answer every question there is about how the product works. This document describes exactly what the product to be built will do. It specifies for whom the product is being built, why it's important it be built, and what ideals should be kept in mind along the way.

The PRD's audience is everyone who is involved in the product development process. The engineering team will use it as a basis for writing their technical design. The QA team will use it as a basis for what to test. The customer support team will use it as a basis for updating their customer support scripts and help center content. The legal team will use it to understand exactly what is being built and what the implications may be. The marketing team will need it to understand what new capabilities they can talk about.

The PRD should not be written by the PM alone in a quiet corner. The process of writing the PRD will be iterative and incorporate the cross-functional working team that is helping to define the product – especially the UX and engineering partners. As I describe the sections of the PRD, I'll also describe the process for how you work with others on the team to build those sections out.

The key sections of the PRD are as follows. You may incorporate additional sections, but these are indispensable:

1. Controls
2. Links
3. Vision / What is being built
4. Why
5. Background
6. Definitions
7. Terms
8. Prioritization
9. Principles
10. Business goals
11. Target users & Personas
12. Eligibility criteria
13. User goals and Journeys
14. Requirements

15. Metrics

There's some content that should not appear in the PRD, which should be written by others, after the PRD is agreed upon.

Importantly, the PRD should not contain any technical design, which specifies *how* the thing will be built by the engineering team. The technical design will be written by the engineering team.

The PRD should also refrain from becoming a project plan, which specifies when and by whom the thing will be built. A project manager should put together a project plan once the PRD is agreed upon by the key stakeholders. When there's no project manager, a PM or tech lead can manage a project plan.

I'll now go into each section of the PRD in detail below.

Metadata & Controls

Add a section to your PRD describing the requirements process itself.

First, who wrote it? When was it authored? Was there a major edit to highlight? For example:

```
Author: Product Manager Jane
Date started: 2025-08-15
Last major revision: 2026-02-15 Accounted for admin
user type
```

Next, what stage is the PRD in? Help the reader understand whether the document is a work in progress, or if the product has already been launched. For example:

```
Stage: Draft | Reviewing | Approved | Development |
Testing | Launched
```

Readers & Approvers

You can also specify who all the reviews and approvers are. When your PRD is authored in a collaboration tool like Google Docs, you may invite your approvers to mark their approval directly in your document. Otherwise, you can get approvals in whatever way works in your organization, and then update the PRD yourself. Readers may be added as FYI, while explicit buy-in from approvers is required to move forward. For example, your headings might be:

- **Function**, which could be Marketing, Legal, Engineering, and so on
- **Person,** for the actual assignment of who will fulfill the review
- **FYI** or **Approver**, to specify what type of read the review should be
- **Read/Approved on**, where the reviewer can initial and date once they've completed their review

Links

As the PRD is often the starting point for learning about a project, add links to other key documents in a predictable spot. Documents you may include are:

- Two-pagers
- Vision documents
- Complete UX mocks
- The technical design document
- The project plan
- The test plan
- The product roadmap

You may not have all these documents when you start the PRD, but you can add links as these documents become available.

Next, let's get into the content of the PRD itself.

Vision / What is being built

The section explains what we're building. Put the product in context. Remember, it's helpful to attach yourself to something bigger. What broader vision is this deliverable a part of?

You may also explain at a high level who you're building for, though you'll go into much more detail in the *Target users* section.

This section should go into as much detail as necessary so the reader, if they stop reading after this section, more or less knows what can be expected as the outcome of the project.

Why

The "why" section is critical and explains why this is an important product to build or problem to solve. All too often, answering *Why?* is an afterthought. *What* and *How* are often answered, but *Why* is often left a mystery.

A solution in search of a problem is a dangerous thing. If you aren't solving a real world problem for real world people, then you can burn an infinite amount of energy and resources building a product that will never achieve your goals or find product market fit.

Start with answering the question *Why* before you go any further. Below are three key questions to answer to establish your Why.

1. Pose a clear *problem statement*. Why is this a problem for the target user? Are you solving a pain point in an existing product or workflow? Are you providing a new capability that wasn't there before? What are users unable to do today? Or are they seeking out maddening workarounds for which your solution simplifies their life?

2. How big of a problem is it? A handy way to measure this is how frequently users encounter the problem, how severe the problem is when they encounter it, and how important users feel it is for this problem to be addressed. The value can also be measured in how much users are willing to pay for a

solution, or how much they are paying today for workarounds in time or money.

3. Why is now the right time to solve the problem? For whatever reason, the problem you propose to solve hasn't been solved yet. Why not? If it was worth solving, surely others would be trying. Has something changed that makes now the right time to solve this problem? Perhaps a new technology is available that wasn't available before; e.g., 5G network speeds or virtual reality goggles. Maybe a new audience is available; e.g., a concept that has been proven out in one country will now be introduced in another country.

Background

The background section contains all the information you need to know – briefly – to understand the problem space. The background section should answer these questions:

- What existing data confirms the problem exists?
- What is the current state of the art?
- Have any solutions already been tried that failed?
- What do we need to know to understand why this solution will succeed?

In the beginning stages of the project, when you're still getting everyone on the same page, the Background section is very helpful. But it can become very long. Once everyone is bought into the work to be done, the Background section can become a big moat that the reader has to cross in order to get to the details about what is to be built. When you feel you're at this stage, you can move this section to an appendix.

Definitions

To ensure everyone understands the PRD in the same way, clarify any new or important definitions up-front. There are two types of definitions that are important. The first is domain-specific terms used within the document that may be unfamiliar to readers. The second is nomenclature used within the document itself, specifically your short-hand for prioritization.

Terms

Even jargon that you think is well known is worth defining in the PRD. This may be industry jargon, acronyms, or code names for projects. The wider the audience for your PRD becomes, the more likely people who are unfamiliar with your team's jargon are to read it. The engineering team may be the first audience, but your company's lawyers are likely to read your PRD when you're seeking launch approval. And years down the road you'll be surprised to find someone from an entirely different part of the company is still reading your PRD to gain insights. Because many people are embarrassed to speak up when they don't know what something means, err on the side of caution by defining any term that may have even the smallest chance of ambiguity or unfamiliarity.

Prioritization

Feature lists can be endless, but time is not. If some features are less important than others, say so. This helps the team focus on the most important work first. I label every aspect of my PRD with three prioritization tiers, and I clearly define those tiers in each PRD so the reader knows exactly what I mean by each.

- **P0:** Must. The product cannot launch without this. These items should be worked on first.
- **P1:** Should. These items should be done, but if the schedule becomes squeezed, it's OK to cut them. These items should be worked on last.
- **P2:** Don't. We've thought about this, but decided it isn't worth the effort to implement. These items *should not be worked on*, even if there's time. A P0/P1 probably exists in some other project and should be addressed first.

It takes a bit of getting used to for a team to actively *ignore* P2 items. Trust me, it's well worth it to have a shorthand for how you say No to features in your PRD, not only a way to say yes. You can opt to be explicit and simply write the words "Don't" in the PRD instead of P2.

Principles

Principles dictate boundaries on how the product should work. For example, "The user's privacy should always be respected."

You may not know what principles will be important at the

start, so this section is unlikely to be written in the first draft of your PRD. Once questions come up during the product development process, suddenly you'll find a need for principles to clarify the decisions that are being made. The engineering team will want to go one way. You want to go the other way. And marketing has another opinion altogether. Who is right?

Because all too often we assume our principles are obvious and are already shared among all our team members, principles are often perilously left out of PRDs. *Obviously the user's privacy should be respected!* Don't assume that everyone on your team shares the same principles, or prioritizes them equally. Have an explicit discussion to get everyone on the same page. Record the principle, and then see how decisions on other parts of the PRD shake out with that new principle in place.

Prioritize your principles from most important to least important. Sometimes principles will be in conflict. When that occurs, it's important to know which one takes precedence.

Goals

The goals should be driven by the *Why* section, which reveals the motivating problem you are trying to address. The project goals should directly state what part of the motivating problem is resolved by doing this work. Goals lead to how the team should measure success.

For example, let's say the problem statement is that charities aren't raising enough money online today. A purpose-driven goal may be to raise $XM for charity online. One of the ways you may raise money online is through a donation widget, which you'll define in detail in your PRD. As a product manager, the goal you define should be about raising money, not about building the widget.

This is a key point. Success is not building the widget to spec. Success is raising money for charity. If the widget, once built, hasn't raised any more money for charity, you would not consider your goals to have been met. So the goal in the PRD *cannot be only to build the widget.*

Think about it in reverse. Here's what happens when you set the goal to be "Add a donation widget to the site" rather than "Raise $10M via on-site donations".

The engineering team builds the donation widget you requested. Fast forward one year and look at the results. The donations report says you raised a measly $10 – a far cry from $10M. Upon further investigation, you learn the $10 came from the QA tester who was verifying the widget worked as per the design in the PRD, and she was refunded for her donation.

The engineering team spent so much time building the donation widget, and you have nothing to show for it. You frantically talk to the engineering lead about the faulty widget. "It didn't raise any money! We were supposed to raise $10M!"

What's her response? "We built it exactly per the design in your PRD. We tested it – it satisfied *the goal you set for us*! We didn't know you wanted to raise $10M. If we had known that, we could have told you a lot sooner that this widget approach would never work."

The engineering lead got a great performance review because she satisfied your request to build the widget, on time and on budget. You got a terrible performance review because you wasted an engineering team's time on a project that had no measurable business impact.

The team needs to have the same shared high-level *business* goals by which all parties measure success of the project.

Remember that goals must be prioritized based on your priority definitions of Must, Should, Won't; or P0, P1, P2; or whatever works for you.

Target users

If your product is for a specific type of user, explain who they are and what their expectations are. Is your target retail, enterprise, government? List all the details that may be relevant to ensuring the user journeys and product requirements are focused for the target user.

Personas or Roles

If there are very specific user classes that will have their own experiences, list and describe them here. For example, children, parents, administrators and guests may all have different roles. Write down what the high level expectations are for each.

Eligibility criteria

If your product only works for a subset of users, explain that here. For example, are you targeting certain platforms like iOS or Android? Certain versions? Do users need to already own another product to make use of yours? Do users need to be a specific age? Do they need to live in a specific country or region?

User goals and journeys

Up to now the work was to convince readers that the problem is worth solving and who we're solving it for. Now we get to the main event of the PRD. The next sections – user goals and journeys, followed by requirements – are interrelated. Here you'll explain exactly what is needed to solve the problem. To get them right, you need to understand how they're related and how they're different.

A user journey is all the steps the user must take to accomplish a *user goal*. A user goal is different from the project goals we set out earlier. While project goals relate to business outcomes, *user goals* specify what the user is coming to your product to accomplish in their own life. When a task is frequent, or when users expect the task to be front-and-center and easy to do, you should define a user journey that creates a smooth experience that enables users to easily accomplish the task, from end-to-end, without having to think about all the disjointed underlying capabilities that make it all possible.

User journeys start by specifying a goal that a user wants to *accomplish* with your product. By clearly stating what user goals should be achievable with the product, you set the stage for making sure the product is designed with those user goals in mind. If you design from the point of view of user goals, the end product will be completely different than if you design from the point of view of features.

Let's explore an example based on photo sharing:

User goal: *"A user can take a photo and immediately send it to a top contact."*
  Journey:

- The user opens the photos app
- After they take a photo, an unobtrusive share button is overlaid on the screen
- Tapping the share button results in top contacts overlaid on the screen
- With a tap of the contact's face the photo is sent

This interface lets a user accomplish their task quickly. It's designed around their goal, not on the underlying components.

It may help to discuss what a user journey is *not*. A user journey is not a description of a user's day. A user journey should not sound like this: "Jane wakes up and decides she wants to send a photo to her friend." So many first-time writers of user journeys write journeys that describe something that is happening in a person's life, how it leads them to a software product, and how that software product saves the day. That is not a user journey.

User journeys are not features or requirements (which will be discussed next). Many people are trained to think in terms of *features*. For example:

- The camera app should have a share *feature*
- The email compose app should have an "attach file" *feature*

Features are not user journeys. When we build in terms of features, it may be possible to do many things, but it may not be *easy* or *intuitive* to achieve the goals. Have you ever tried to do something in an app or website, but you couldn't find the thing you were looking for? Fairly frequently, I encounter websites where the navigation is so bad that the fastest way to do something is to Google how to do it.

Often Google brings me to an article that describes the unintuitive steps to accomplish the task. What seems like it should be a connected sequence of steps actually has to be done as a disjointed series of steps in multiple places. Technically, the thing you want to do is possible by hopping around to the right "features" one by one, but accomplishing the task isn't easy or intuitive.

How might the photo sharing goal look without an explicit user journey?

Let's start with all the components involved. There's the phone's camera/photo feature. The photos typically get stored on the phone in a photo browsing app. There is a contacts app on the phone. And there are apps to send stuff around, such as SMS, email, etc.

139

In a strictly component-based view of the world, the following might be required to send a photo to a contact:

- Open the camera app and take a photo
- Open the email app and start composing a message
- Start typing the email address and select the contact
- Find the "attach file" feature
- Navigate to select a photo instead of a file
- Find the photo
- Select it
- Attach it
- Send the email

Yes, sharing a photo was possible with this series of steps, but it certainly wasn't easy.

The process of designing user journeys

Typically the process of writing user goals and journeys is iterative. A PRD is not typically written from end-to-end in a single sitting, because product design is a collaborative process. You need a starting point that you use to gather feedback.

Here's how this collaborative process might unfold.

First, the PM should write the high level user goals and review and refine them with the team – especially the UX and engineering leads.

Next, the UX team comes up with an experience design for how the user can accomplish those goals. The UX team proposes flows in the form of wireframes or mockups. The product manager must verify that the goals are actually met by the proposed user experience; and the engineering team should be involved to consult on the feasibility of the design.

If you don't have UX resources at your disposal, you can draw the user journeys by hand and take photos. Do not skip this step – a picture says a thousand words.

Once the team is aligned on how the user goals will be accomplished through UX design, the PM should incorporate the UX mocks into the PRD. The mocks explain visually how each use goal is achieved in the product. Pairing design mocks with a text description is essential. The PM should write text enumerating the steps a user takes to get from start to finish in accomplishing the goal. This painstaking process of describing the paths to accomplish user goals is also how you ensure all cases are fully covered.

Start with the primary journey – i.e., what happens when everything goes right. Then enumerate all the edge cases – i.e., all the ways things could go wrong and how the user either exits the flow or resolves the problem.

Some "edge cases" may be big enough to warrant their own user journey altogether. For example, allowing the user to send a photo they just took to someone who is not yet a contact might be complicated enough to warrant being its own user journey. Is it a user goal you will handle in the flow of taking the photo, or will the user have to exit the camera app and add the contact in the contacts app? These are the sorts of questions you want to think through and resolve while iterating on the user goals and journeys.

Because user journeys follow the experience from the user perspective, they provide absolutely critical information to the cross-functional team. The customer support and QA teams will look to understand what users are expected to do with the product. The legal team will look here to understand the implications of the product launch. So on and so forth.

Prioritize your user journeys. P0s are your *critical user journeys,* or CUJs. The critical journeys are required for the MVP. The P1s are nice to have.

> *User Experience Designers are critical partners for Product Managers*
>
> When many people think of "UX", they mistakenly think of the "look and feel" of a product. The look and feel is actually the *visual design* (often called "VisD"). UX, on the other hand, is the *experience* a user lives through in order to accomplish their tasks in your product. UX is not static like VisD, or describable via a style guide. The UX encompasses the sequences users work through to actually use the product. The UX is the sum-total of all the user-journeys, planned and unplanned. A product can live or die on the user experience it creates.

Requirements

User journeys are difficult for many people to master, because we typically don't encounter them until we begin working in product roles. Even then, it can take a long time to fully understand what they are and how they're different from product requirements.

User journeys describe what goals users can accomplish, and do so in a linear narrative that may jump from one software component to the next.

The requirements section, on the other hand, should comprehensively specify exactly how each component will behave under every set of circumstances. Rather than tracing a user's path through completing an action, requirements should be broken down by product component or capability, whatever makes sense in your case.

In our photo sharing example, the requirements section might be broken down into four sections:

1. Camera screen
2. Contact selection
3. Messaging app selection
4. Settings

The user journeys may take their own winding paths through these four components, touching on different aspects of each. In the requirements section of the PRD, you enumerate the sum total of all necessary changes to each component, one component at a time.

You can think of the user journeys section as explaining the product from the user's perspective, while the requirements section explains the product from the product developer's perspective. When determining how much engineering effort will be required, it's the requirements that come in most handy. But the user journeys are absolutely indispensable to making sure the completed product can truly do what was intended.

Imagine a scenario where the engineering team is short on time and wants to cut features to launch on time. If all you have are the requirements, you don't know how the product is intended to be used. A requirement that is crucial to the user goals may not seem very important without the context of the user journeys to clarify its value.

The requirements are necessary to estimate how long it will take to develop a product.

Metrics

How will you measure success? What are the key performance indicators of the product? Enumerating what you want to measure and any way you want to slice the data will help the data science team and engineering team establish the right instrumentation and build the right dashboards.

Project plan

The project plan lays out all the work to be done. Depending on the team dynamics, the project plan may be owned by the product manager, the eng manager, or a project manager. I hope you're lucky enough to be working with a project manager who can maintain the project plan.

There are many tools out there to make project tracking easier. Some examples are Jira, Asana, and Smartsheet. There are always new tools entering the market. Whether you choose to use one of these tools, or simply use a spreadsheet is up to you. Perhaps shockingly, at Google we used simple spreadsheets more often than we used any tools. The basic information a project plan tracks is the same regardless of the tool you use. If your plan is in a spreadsheet, label columns with each of the following bits of data:

- Priority
- Title
- Owner
- Status
- Effort, Expected start and end
- Depends on
- Links
- Notes

The project plan should also be broken down into Milestones. I'll describe each of these in more detail below:

Priority

How important is this item? Use the standard priorities described in the PRD (P0, P1), or Must, Should. In a project plan, there's no need to write down what you *won't* do, which was done in the PRD.

Title

The title is a succinct description for each work item that you and others will understand.

Owner

Who is responsible for getting this task done? Always look for opportunities to assign tasks to others. It's tempting to take on many things yourself, but you won't be able to scale your impact if you're involved in too many low-level tasks yourself. Try to take yourself out of the critical path whenever possible. Think of assigning tasks as giving others opportunities and challenges.

Status

Where is this item in its life cycle? Come up with a list of status types that make sense for your project. If in doubt, try using these: Not started, In progress, Done, Verified, Blocked, Canceled. In the next section on *Plan Item Statuses*, I'll go into more detail on what each of these means.

Effort, Expected start and Expected end

Your project plan should have some way of noting when a task can or will begin, and when it's expected to end. One way of doing this is to explicitly write both dates. Another is to have a level-of-effort estimate and derive the end date based on the start date and how long the task is expected to take. T-shirt sizes like S, M, L, XL can be used as a shorthand, and you can roughly translate the T-shirt size to a number of weeks.

Project management software may take care of these calculations for you. In a simple or small project, working out these dates by hand in a spreadsheet may be easy enough.

Depends on

This task may require another task to be completed before it can begin. In this case, you can list the items here, so you can remind yourself not to bother checking the status of this task until its dependencies have been met.

If adding a *Depends on* column, be sure you have a simple way to refer to other items in the spreadsheet. You can't use row numbers because those may change as the project evolves, or if you change the sort order of the project plan.

What you can do is add another column, *ID*, to store a unique identifier that can be used for reference in other places. Again, this is something that project management software will take care of for you. Most tools will also create a Gantt chart, which can show you a visual timeline of your project, taking

147

dependencies into account.

Link(s) to document

Linking documents to your plan helps the team understand progress. Having a link to mocks says loudly and clearly, "we have mocks!" It also makes the project plan an invaluable index from which the team can get to a project's key documents.

Notes

A notes column in the project plan allows you to take notes regarding the status updates themselves. For example, if an item is delayed for a week, the notes column is a good place to document that. Be sure to include the date when each note was written.

Breaking down the status column

It's worth going into a bit more detail about the *Status* column. I like to track the following statuses, but you can choose whatever makes sense for your workflow.

- Not started
- In progress
- Done
- Verified
- Blocked
- Canceled

Not started

This is the default state that every task's status starts as.

In progress

The task should be in this state when it's actually being worked on. Being assigned is not sufficient to move a task into this status. That is a common mistake that leads to a project looking like many pieces are in motion when in reality they aren't. When a task is assigned, set the owner. When the owner reports they have actually started work, change the status to *In progress*.

Done

When the owner reports they're done, this is the appropriate status.

Verified

Depending on your workflow, you may have a verification step. QA will test the features an engineer has reported as done and move the item to Verified if the tests pass.

Blocked

Blocked means that you can't make progress until something else happens.

It's important to know when the team is blocked, because

THE PRODUCT MANAGER'S GUIDE

it's the PM's job to help the team get unblocked. That could mean tracking down approvals, securing additional resources, clarifying problematic requirements, etc.

Canceled

If an item is no longer needed, setting the status to *canceled* makes that clear. It's better to set the status to *canceled* rather than delete the item, as doing so provides additional details about how the project evolved over time. You may find the information useful when you return to the project plan months down the road. Be sure to take notes when an item is canceled.

Milestones

It's useful to break a plan down into milestones so you can see progress along the way. A milestone might mark some set of useful functionality that's fully usable. A great way to declare milestones is when some set of user journeys is ready for testing.

Beware of defining milestones based on a layer of engineering work that's complete. If there's nothing testable from a product experience perspective, then the milestone is not particularly useful.

Imagine a project with two user journeys, *A* and *B*. Both have back-end and front-end work. The eng team may consider that they are 50% done with the work if they've completed 100% of the back-end work. They may propose a milestone called "Back-end work complete". Unfortunately, although 50% of the work is theoretically complete, 0% of the user journeys are testable.

It's much better for your first milestone to encompass Journey A being end-to-end complete, including the front-end and back-end work and any integration work and testing required. The next milestone can be for Journey B being end-to-end complete. Tracked this way, at the conclusion of each milestone, you can actually use the functionality that's been built, get a feel for it, and figure out if it works well or not.

In the layer-by-layer approach, you may find that you need to complete the entire project before you can start testing any of your product. That's risky because it makes it very difficult to course correct away from a problematic design, or catch usability issues early on. It often undercounts integration time.

On the other hand, if each milestone delivers usable functionality, it's possible to spot when something doesn't work how you intended early in the process. Fixing design flaws early – especially user experience design flaws – results in a much greater chance of success.

Some will notice that in its focus on usable deliverables at the end of each milestone, what I'm describing above bears close resemblance to "sprint"-oriented agile development. I'm not a rigid advocate of any methodology in particular – only that the best practices be used. Agreeing on how you'll structure milestones or whether you'll use a predefined methodology to organize the team's efforts must be agreed to with your engineering partners.

Roadmap

The roadmap is a high level timeline. A roadmap could describe a single project and be a zoomed out version of your project plan. More likely, a roadmap zooms out even further and describes how a series of projects fit together over a longer period to achieve a bigger vision. The roadmap starts with where you are now and it ends with your larger vision being realized. Key milestones that lead toward your vision being achieved are roughly fixed to future dates.

The timeline of a high level roadmap should be divided in quarters or halves, if not years. The roadmap describes only major milestones or key delivered work. Individual work items, which may be measured in days or weeks, do not belong in a roadmap. Work items belong in a *project plan for the individual projects*.

In addition to the timeline, a good roadmap document will have the following basic metadata:

- The project name
- The project goal(s)
- The time bounds of all the projects
- The names of the teams or leads responsible for the project
- The date when the roadmap was last updated

Here is a single project's launch roadmapped out over four quarters. This is more like a "high level project plan" than a true roadmap, but useful nonetheless. A snapshot like this provides your stakeholders with an at-a-glance way to understand when your project will launch and how you'll get there. Without this, they might grossly underestimate how long it will take for you to complete your project, at no fault of theirs. A high level timeline / roadmap like the one below helps you manage expectations.

Q1'22
    Complete PRD
    Run focus group user research study with clickable UX prototype
    Complete technical design

Q2'22
    Engineering development completed
    QA passed
    Go To Market plan defined

Q3'22
    Launch end-user experiments and fine-tune parameters
    Launch to all users
    Execute GTM

Q4'22
    Follow-up on success metrics

More often, a roadmap will be higher level, describing a series of launches, not focusing on the specifics mechanics of the launches themselves. Here's an example of the progression of an online multiplayer game with a 3rd party marketplace for weapons and clothing. The game isn't released all at once, but lands over the course of two years. The MVP comes out far in advance of the complete vision.

H1'22
   Launch MVP: single-player monster shooter game

H2'22
   Launch online multiplayer mode

2023
   Launch in-app store for purchasing weapons and clothing

2024
   Launch 3P marketplace

A roadmap like the one above allows for market validation of each phase of the product before further investment.

In the example below, the roadmap below shows a progression of releasing the same product in different regions. Internationalizing a product is a lot of work. In addition to translations, ensuring legal compliance, making sure it's easy for users to pay in the local currencies and other considerations can make international rollouts tricky.

H1'22
   US launch

H2'22
   English- language launches in UK, CA, AU, IE, SA

2023

EMEA launches

2024
Rest of world launch

Use a Roadmap for staffing

The roadmap that contains goals fixed to a timeline helps communicate your intention to stakeholders who are eager for your product to be delivered as well as those who control the purse strings.

The roadmap is the first venue where you can have a conversation and negotiation about the timeline and resourcing. Your engineering lead might say, "You want to finish this by Q3? There's no way with the size of the team we have now..." Then the fun begins to negotiate for more time (if the deadline was imposed externally), more resources, or reducing the scope of the project.

It's often said that in software development, there are three variables – time, features, and cost – and you can only control for two of them. Cost is typically measured in the number of engineers and supporting functions working to build the project. That means that if you have a fixed number of engineers and a fixed amount of time, you may have to sacrifice some features to launch on time. If you can't sacrifice any features and your team size is also fixed, then you'll have to accept going slower. And finally, if you have a firm launch date and the feature set isn't negotiable, then you either need more resources, or you have to find ways to do more with less.

Running a meeting

Running a productive meeting is an art. Ensuring that a meeting moves a project forward requires planning for the meeting in advance, managing the meeting while it's happening, and following up on people's commitments afterwards. You can't just put a bunch of people in a room and hope for the best. At minimum, you need to establish a clear goal for the group you've assembled.

In this section, I'll present ten tips for ensuring your meetings are highly productive, followed by a sample meeting agenda that can be used to organize the meeting goals, take notes, and record action items.

Ten tips for running a successful meeting

Here are the ten tips, which I'll dive into one by one:

1. Ensure the meeting has a clear owner
2. Have a clear goal
3. Invite the right people
4. Send the agenda out in advance
5. Allot and track time
6. Keep the meeting on track
7. Take notes
8. Assign action items with clear deliverables and deadlines
9. Send notes out after the meeting
10. Follow-up on action items

Ensure the meeting has a clear owner

Typically the person who sends out the meeting is the de facto owner. But what does it mean to own a meeting? In exchange for people's time, you ensure that the meeting will be productive and achieve its goals. You prepare in advance so no one's time is wasted. During the meeting, you manage the discussion to keep it on track, and ensure all critical topics get covered. And you follow up after the meeting to ensure commitments are kept and momentum is maintained.

Have a clear goal

You should have a clear goal for your meeting. To be successful, everyone needs to know what that goal is. If you don't have a goal, you probably shouldn't be having a meeting. "Status updates" is a terrible goal because it lacks a clear sense of what outcome is expected. Don't be surprised if you find it hard to identify a meeting goal; most people do, which is why there are so many bad meetings in this world. A great way to identify a meeting goal is to answer the question: *What is the next key deliverable that will move this project forward?*

Invite the right people

Meetings with too many people are not productive – at least not for the vast majority of the people who are invited. The key to knowing who should be invited is being clear on the meeting's goal. The more amorphous the goal, the less clarity you'll have on who should be invited, and the greater the tendency to invite more and more people, ultimately wasting more of people's time.

Having a laser focused meeting goal doesn't mean you should invite very *few* people. It means you can now invite the *right* people. Include anyone whose knowledge or opinion matters to resolve the issues. When it's not clear, you can ask. For example, if you need a marketing person and you don't have someone on point for your project already, you can ask the head of marketing, "Who on your team can join meetings on project X to speak for marketing on our goal to accomplish Z?" Doing this gives the marketing lead the option to join themselves, or to delegate to someone on their team. It relieves you from inviting the entire marketing team.

Send the agenda out in advance

As part of a daily wrap-up routine, I'll look through tomorrow's calendar. For any meetings that I'm running, I'll ensure there's an agenda with a clear stated goal. If I can't think of one, I cancel the meeting. Otherwise I update the agenda, review the attendees and send out the meeting agenda with a request for input ahead of the meeting.

At its core, an agenda is a list of topics to be covered during the meeting. But simply covering a meandering list of topics is often not super useful. I also recommend embedding the meeting goal into the agenda so everyone is on the same page regarding why they're there from the start. All of the agenda items should fit under the goal. You can assign owners to individual agenda items so they know you expect them to lead that part of the discussion.

To give the meeting participants a chance to get mentally prepared for your meeting, send them the agenda in advance. You can also invite participants to add suggestions for additional agenda items or add meeting notes ahead of time. Whatever tool you use for keeping agendas and notes, make sure all meeting participants have access to edit so they can participate actively in the pre-meeting phase. It may be tempting to send out a short email with a link to your agenda doc. I prefer to lower the bar to reading the agenda by copying my agenda into the email. I still provide the link so participants can add to the agenda, but I don't require them to click and open up a document in order to see what I have planned.

Allot and track time

Thankfully, meetings are not infinite. You want to be sure you can accomplish the meeting's goal in the time you've scheduled, whether 30 or 60 minutes. If you can accomplish the goal in a shorter amount of time, then shorter is always better! Don't waste people's time.

A good way to do this is to note directly into the agenda how much time you plan to spend on each section. By doing this ahead of the meeting, you have a gut-check of whether you have enough time to cover the topics you need to cover, or if you have too many topics for the allotted time. If you don't have enough time, you may need to focus the meeting more sharply, so there's ample time for the most critical topics. When allocating time, remember that a 30 minute meeting doesn't really have 30 minutes. The first 3-5 minutes are going to be spent on assembling the group, getting everyone settled, and having polite chit-chat. The last few minutes should be reserved for reviewing action items and next steps. And you should expect every topic is going to go over its allotted time, so build in buffers. With that in mind, plan for no more than 20-25 minutes of content in a 30 minute meeting.

Keep the meeting on track

By setting time bounds on each topic, you've also advertised your expectations to the group. This gives you permission to end discussion and move on to the next topic. You can say something like "This is a really good discussion, but we've got some other key areas to address, so let's start wrapping up on this topic." Of course, you can't just abruptly curtail discussion of an important topic. You have to provide some kind of closure. This could mean setting up a dedicated meeting to do a deeper dive into a topic that clearly needed its own meeting. It could mean asking someone to take an action item to do a deep dive on a topic and report back to the team.

Sometimes people go off on tangents and stray far from the topic or meeting purpose. You need to develop ways to bring people back from tangents. For example, "Let's not design the solution in this meeting – let's stick to outcome definitions here." Or, "That's a really important discussion to have, but can I ask you to link up with so-and-so and come up with a proposal offline?"

Take notes

What happened in a meeting is quickly forgotten unless you memorialize it in notes. You don't always have to be the note-taker, but you should be sure someone is taking notes. If there is a project manager involved in your project, they are a great candidate because they are likely to be following up on most of the AIs that get recorded in the notes, anyway.

If there's nothing else being presented during the meeting, present the meeting notes so everyone in the meeting can see them. That gives the group an opportunity to review and correct the notes while they're being written. It also helps people get back on track quickly if their attention was diverted momentarily.

Assign action items with clear deliverables and deadlines

Whenever the group identifies something that needs to be done – an *action item*, or *AI* – it must have a clear owner and deadline. It's all too common to see a group of five people agree in a meeting, "We should really do X." Everyone nods their heads in agreement, and then the group moves on to the next agenda item. While everyone agrees X should be done, no one knows who is responsible to do it. As the meeting owner, you should ensure that every action identified has a clear owner. You can say, "Before we move on, let's make sure there's a clear owner for X. Jessica, can you take that on?" And just as importantly, set a clear deadline: "Can you send a draft to this group by next Tuesday, so we can all review it before our next meeting?"

161

Send notes out after the meeting

Sending out the notes after a meeting accomplishes two goals. First, it spreads the information beyond the group that was present. Your distribution list for meeting notes can be broader than just the group who was invited to the meeting. The distribution list can contain people who need an FYI but don't need to spend their time in the meeting itself.

Second, sending out notes reminds everyone of their AIs. Rather than have AIs only embedded in the notes where they came up chronologically, I suggest collecting them in a clearly labeled list so everyone can quickly see what they're responsible for.

Follow-up on action items

When action items have clear owners and clear delivery dates, it's straightforward to follow up on them. While preparing the agenda for the follow-up meeting, you can review the previous meeting's AIs and send quick notes to action item owners. There's a fine line between a quick check in and nagging, but if done well, most people will be thankful for a reminder. No one wants to show up to the next meeting having completely forgotten about their tasks.

Meeting agenda & notes template

I find it easiest to manage a single running document with all the meetings for a given project. Before each meeting, create an agenda of the meeting topics, and then use the same document to take notes during the meeting. Give each meeting its own dated heading so you know when the meeting happened and what kind of meeting it was.

> *{date} - {meeting title}*
> Attendees: Joe L., Jessica K., Steve R., Dan C.
> Agenda:
> Review of project goals - Dan - 1 min
> Goal: Find a way forward on blockers in workstream X:
> Blocker 1 - Steve - 8 min
> Blocker 2 - Jessica - 8 min
> Blocker 3 - Joe - 8 min
> Next steps:
> Ensure blockers are resolved in next meeting
> Loop in QA to test all resolved areas
> Action items (AIs):
> AI: Steve to check with Robin if ...
> AI: Jessica to work with Franz on ..., target next week for resolution
> AI: Joe to escalate database failures issue to eng prod team

6

Process

Under the comb
the tangle and the straight path
are the same.
—Heraclitus, Fragments

There are typically far more options than there is time and bodies to implement every great idea. Process is key to prioritize ideas and work.

Before jumping headlong into discussing how process can help you, I want to first acknowledge that "process" is a high-voltage word. The word is often associated with bureaucracy, and too much process without good reason can definitely be a bad thing. A common refrain from stretched-thin employees in large companies is, "there's too much process!" Teams can get bogged down, unable to make rapid progress because they're required to do a lot of things that feel unnecessary in order to do the things that feel important.

But process, when used correctly, can be a source of power. Writing down the process provides for repeatability for common team activities or product operations. Whenever something needs to be done in the expected way more than once, establishing a process helps ensure that it gets done regardless of who is doing the job.

Process can also help teams work more efficiently and paradoxically make progress happen faster. An established process gives a clear guide on how to continue moving forward and make progress. Without a defined process, every time a group gets together to do something, they have to first establish their own ground rules. A process that can be followed lets the group focus on completing the task rather than the meta work of how they'll complete it. An especially important part of any process definition is specifying who has authority to approve and make decisions. When it comes to slowing a team down, unclear decision making is far worse than extra process steps.

Process can actually be the basis for innovation that leads to competitive advantage. As such, it's one of *Doblin's 10 Types of Innovation*. Says Doblin: "Process innovations involve the activities and operations that produce an enterprise's primary offerings. Innovating here requires a dramatic change from 'business as usual' that enables the company to use unique capabilities, function efficiently, adapt quickly, and build market–leading margins. Process innovations often form the core competency of an enterprise, and may include patented or proprietary approaches that yield advantages for years or even decades. They can be the 'special sauce' you use that competitors simply can't replicate."

The most famous example in the realm of process power is Toyota. Dubbed "The Toyota Way," their process enabled Toyota to build high quality cars more efficiently than the competition, making them the most valuable car company in the world before they were unseated by Tesla. Their process was so ingrained in their culture and corporate ethos that it was nearly impossible to copy, even though Toyga actually trained executives of competing automakers in The Toyota Way.

But let's start with the basics that revolve around the product:

- How does the team align on what to work on next? (See Planning cycles, below)
- How does the team build the product features? (See Execution, above)
- Once launched, are there any human-driven processes that are required for the product to deliver value to users? (aka, product operations)
- How do you manage problems that are found in the product itself once users are using it? (See Issue Triage, below)

Planning cycles

An ideal team process involves spending some time planning, and then spending some time doing. A manager of mine once said, "Plan the work, then work the plan."

Some teams constantly thrash, upending goals and changing priorities constantly. In such a work environment, it can be challenging to get anything out the door. The team's patience may wear thin if everything they build gets scrapped before it sees the light of day. Setting a plan and sticking to it helps maintain a sense of stability.

Meanwhile, situations change, and it's important to be nimble and responsive. So how often should you kick off a planning cycle, and how much work should you bite off at once?

Ideally you can establish an outlook as far into the future as possible, with an explicit understanding that the further out the outlook, the less certain you'll actually adhere to the plan. There should be some unit of time where the team can feel the plan won't change under their feet. The right length of time for such a commitment depends on the maturity of your team/product and your market. In a mature team, you may plan yearly goals and stick to them; in a startup, even quarterly goals may feel like they are looking exceedingly far in the future. The key is to pick a period of time that gives you enough time to do something meaningful, but not so long that the world is likely to have changed dramatically before you're through the cycle.

Regardless of the cycle length you choose, the process is going to follow a similar pattern.

- First, you align on goals.
- Next, you prioritize those goals.
- Finally, you staff the work.

Planning is, in many ways, a continuous process. If you're

planning annual goals, chances are you still need half-year and quarterly planning in order to come up with interim goals and milestones to ensure progress is being made along the way. It's near-impossible to have high fidelity on a plan that spans more than a quarter; so stopping at least quarterly to crisp up exactly what will be done in the next cycle to stay on track is essential. Taking regular pauses to reflect on the plan can reveal if assumptions about a project's complexity or its value were off; if so, the direction can be adjusted.

Goals

Coming up with goals is usually not a problem for teams. Goals can come from many sources. First, the high level product vision typically generates an endless list of potential activities to undertake. Second, goals may also be generated from customer requests. And third, the team itself is likely to have lots of great ideas for what the company can do to get ahead. Gathering up all these goals is step one.

Prioritization

Step two is prioritizing the long list. You obviously can't do everything on the list. If you could, your goals are probably not ambitious enough.

Product managers take the lead in prioritizing product work, with buy-in from the rest of the team. The result of prioritization is that not everything makes the cut. Saying no is something product managers need to get good at. Often you hear the phrase "ruthless prioritization". But the way to politely say no is to say it through a transparent process everyone can participate in. And, through prioritization, rather than a hard "no", you can deliver a softer "not now."

This begs the question: How do you know what to prioritize? When two customers each want their own feature request badly — who gets serviced first? The prioritization process will be infinitely more successful if you can come up with an objective way to prioritize requests.

Having a "north star" metric that you are trying to move helps to align efforts behind having an impact on the metric. If your north star is product engagement, then new features that drive engagement would be prioritized, as would be fixing bugs that impede it. If your northstar is sharing on the platform, then new features that drive sharing would be prioritized, as would be fixing bugs that impede it. Once you have an agreed upon north star, the prioritization exercise then becomes an exercise in estimating how each feature request or bug to be fixed will impact the north star, and at what cost.

As a PM, you have influence over the product direction, and you may be tempted to cut goals you don't like early in the process. Instead, let me suggest that all potential goals survive until the process itself cuts them out. The people who offered the goals you would cut will appreciate that you gave their horse a fair chance in the race.

The team should agree upon a way of measuring the value of any given initiative so everyone can understand how the prioritization that is ultimately arrived at came to be. If you don't have such a "north star metric" already, create one. Although the CEO or some other key person may have the authority to literally dictate what the team works on, in practice that will lead to the team feeling like they don't have much control over their own work. Being able to clearly state that the work is prioritized based on likelihood of generating revenue, or based on frequency of user request gives anyone a shot at contributing to the direction and gives the prioritization legitimacy.

Fulfilling some secondary criteria, such as "It's fun for users" may be equally worthwhile in small amounts, and can impact secondary metrics like retention and your Net Promoter Score (NPS).

You should come out of the prioritization step with a clear ranking of the potential work. Teams often start by prioritizing based on buckets such as High, Medium, Low; or Must do, Should do, and Nice to have. That's a good way to start, and results in a very rough prioritization. But it's often the case that even within the *Must do* list, there's far more than the team can handle. Take that top list and prioritize within it. This is critical for the staffing step to succeed. Start with the number 1 and continue until all the *Must do* items have been ranked.

Having a clear prioritization helps the team make important decisions throughout the work cycle. If a team member needs direction on how to allocate their own time throughout the quarter, they have no further to look than the quarterly stack rank. Stack ranking can also be helpful in uncovering information and getting the team on the same page. As such, it's a process that should not be done alone, but with other team leaders. When leaders disagree on the relative importance of goals, it often means they have a different conception of the goal, the work, or the expected outcome. The stack ranking exercise provides a space for the conversation, which often helps ensure critical information is shared between team members, and information that was assumed to be common knowledge is actually brought out into the open.

Staffing

Once the goals have been prioritized, the next step is for leaders of teams that do the work to roughly scope the amount of work to be done and assign staff to the projects. Typically this refers to the engineering and UX teams, but other teams are often involved as well.

Team leads may roughly classify projects as Small, Medium, Large; or assign a number of weeks that the work will take. Whatever method is chosen, it should ultimately lead to employee-weeks, so the actual weeks the team has during the planned development cycle can be allotted. For example, if you're planning quarterly goals, then you have approximately 12 weeks to spend per employee on the goals, minus time set aside for holidays, vacation, and overhead taken up by meetings and other company distractions. Typically these activities shave off at least 30-40% of each employee's time before you even start allocating them to projects. So for a twelve-week quarter, you'd allocate an employee to a maximum of seven to eight project weeks.

Often, when staff allocation has been completed, the team may be surprised that there are still many Must do's that didn't get staffed. That's why it's so important to have a stack rank ahead of time. You want to be sure that none of the nice-to-haves are taking precedence before all of the musts have been accounted for.

Don't be surprised if another round of prioritization is necessary when projects are cut based on the staffing capacity. Team members may have been accommodating during the prioritization exercise if they thought getting scored as a *Must do* was enough to ensure their favorite project would get staffed. Once they see that isn't sufficient, they'll suddenly become energized and fight harder for their project to rise in the stack rank.

Issue triage

The above process is great for new initiatives. How do you handle ongoing quality work in an already launched product?

Despite the team's best efforts, your product is going to have issues that cause users pain. The issues may be software bugs — i.e., software coding errors that cause an application to crash. The issues may be more subtle, like a failure to properly handle an edge case that wasn't thought of during product development. The product may also be hard or confusing to use, causing challenges for users who can't figure out how to do the things they're supposed to be able to do.

When customers have problems, complaints will come in from

a variety of channels:

- calls or emails to support
- reviews left in app stores
- internal dogfood testers filing bug reports
- friends & family sending emails to employees
- strangers sending you messages on LinkedIn (really!)

If you don't have a system in place for how you manage issue reports, one of two things will naturally happen. Either issues will be completely ignored, which is to your and your users' detriment; or, the squeakiest wheel will get the grease, meaning the most critical issues may not be the ones getting attention.

You'll need to develop a process to ensure issues get triaged for impact and severity and are prioritized appropriately for fixing. The ideal process gets input from all of these diverse channels, and funnels them into a single place — often a bug or issue tracker — where they can be prioritized. The tool you use doesn't matter, so long as you have one, and it's easy for your team to use it.

To have an effective process, consider the following guidelines:

Track issues, not solutions

Issues tracked should correspond to user outcomes and user problems: "User should be able to X, but they aren't able to under circumstance Y." A common trap is for the issue

173

recorded in the tracker to be a technical solution, rather than the user problem: "Fix the database sync issue between components A & B."

You may be asking yourself why this distinction is important; isn't it good to think ahead to the solution? Imagine what happens in this scenario:

An engineer team picks up the issue "Fix the database sync issue between components A & B." The engineer solves the sync issue, marks the task done, and gets a promotion for a job well done.

To your surprise, the customer support team is still reporting "User can't do X in situation Y!" That's impossible, you think, because the eng team fixed the sync issue. Well, maybe the eng team's initial guess at the problem was incorrect. When you track the solution instead of the problem, you lose your grasp on why the work was being done in the first place. Always track the journey that you want to test once the fixes are in place, not the fixes themselves.

Single triage point

If the issues from each channel are tracked separately, it will be very difficult to prioritize across the channels. Find some way for all the channels to converge. If you can't do it automatically, find a low-overhead way to do it manually.

For example, ask the owner of each channel to share their top ten issues in a spreadsheet. The channel owner can do their own triage and sorting of the issues they're aware of. Then you, as the overall owner, can merge the issues from each channel together into a single spreadsheet. That spreadsheet gives you a tractable way to prioritize across all of the channels.

Triage regularly

To keep product quality high, you'll have to triage issues regularly. How regularly depends on your overall product cycles. You may need to triage as frequently as weekly, or as infrequently as quarterly.

A complex cross-channel prioritization like the one I suggested above may be an exercise best suited as part of a quarterly planning exercise. On the other hand, if you have a backlog of bugs you need to get under control, sixty minutes of weekly triage over the course of many weeks may be needed just to sort through the backlog.

Don't triage alone

PMs lead through influence, so they are constantly working toward buy-in from their teams. The easiest way to lose buy-in is to make decisions on your own and announce them to the team. The easiest way to get buy-in on your prioritization is to work through it with others.

Include your channel stakeholders and your eng leads in triage. The channel stakeholders gave you their top-ten prioritization for their channel. They're going to be upset if you change the order of their items without consulting them. They're also going to be less than thrilled if all of their issues fall lower in priority than those from another channel.

By working through triage with others, they have an opportunity to speak to the importance of their issues. Together it's easier to clarify questions and come to a mutually agreed upon prioritization.

Make time for Fit & Finish

Triaging issues is of little value if you never prioritize fixing them. Teams need to come to a consensus on how they'll prioritize fixing issues. One option is to dedicate 10% of the team's time to chugging through the backlog. Another is to sign up to fix specific issues in each development cycle.

7

Influence

Before we get started, let me ask you a series of question:

1. Can you manage a room of senior stakeholders? A room of peers? A room of individual contributors?
2. Are you able to bring a team through the process of making a difficult decision? Do you have a toolkit of frameworks you can draw on to drive decision making? Can you make up a framework on the fly as needed? Can you sell the result to leadership?
3. Do you know how you would leverage a cross-functional team through the complete project life cycle? Do you know how to keep everyone focused?

The product manager is a change agent within an organization. Their job is to build consensus around new initiatives, to get those initiatives properly prioritized and staffed, and to keep teams excited about the process all through development and launch. Product Management is a key role because the product manager focuses the work to be done so it brings the company maximum value, and motivates the rest of the team to do the work.

Product Management is leveraged work, meaning the product manager's impact is scaled based on the number of people who work on the product manager's projects. Even when no one reports to the product manager and they are considered to be an *individual contributor* (or IC), the product manager is nonetheless looked to by the team for direction and answers. This situation poses unique challenges.

In most organizations, the teams that do the work don't report to the product manager. No one has to follow the product manager's decisions because the product manager is not their boss. Rather, the product manager leads the team through influence. Influence requires a mix of being on the right track, being confident but humble, being visible and being liked. People follow you when they like the looks of where you're going and they want to go there with you. A leader is not a leader until someone follows.

I'll talk about influence at three levels. The first level is the art of *Alignment*, or getting buy-in across the organization for the projects you're working to launch. The product manager's work is only valuable if they can get project sponsors to agree that initiatives should be undertaken, and then get teams to agree to do the work.

The second level comes during Execution, when you're working with the cross-functional team to get the product built. Especially if you've never been the leader in the room, it can be intimidating to suddenly be in that role with so many experts in each function looking to you for direction. We can take it for granted that everyone wants the best outcome, but how do you harness the team's passion and expertise? As you'll see, aside from all the skills required to envision and define a project, social, emotional, and communication skills are necessary to build a following and build momentum. Without these skills, you'll have a hard time getting others in the organization to buy into your vision, or to follow you on the journey to achieving it.

The third level is mastering how to manage yourself. There's so much to learn and do in product management, you'll be much more successful in all of it if you have a practice of self-reflection and are skilled in self-management.

Let's dive in.

Alignment

A friend who had recently switched into a product role from engineering management came to me, confused. He said, "My boss gave me this project. Now I'm the product manager for it. He said, go get buy-in. I'm completely stuck." I asked my friend what challenges he was having getting buy-in. He said, "That's the thing. My boss *gave me the project*. Doesn't that mean I have buy-in already? Who am I supposed to get buy-in *from?*"

My answer: "Everyone."

In reality, you'll need to get buy-in from anyone who works on your project, or who will need to approve your project before it can launch.

Once at Google, I led a project that changed the way the Android networking behaved for cellular operators like Google Fi, where I led product for Fi's network. This project took two years from start to finish. A lot of my team's future plans hinged on this project's success. But just before launch, the work was nearly scrapped.

A senior vice-president who was not aware of our project was surprised when his Android phone behaved in an unfamiliar way, he assumed it was a bug. He emailed around asking for this "bug" to be fixed before the Android OS ship date. Emails were sent down the chain until we got the gut-wrenching message: "Please remove these changes before launch."

The senior vice president was doing the right thing. He needed to be sure Android looked the way he expected it to look before it shipped. It's not that our work was bad. It's that the SVP wasn't familiar with it. Lack of familiarity equated to *bug*, and in that moment, it spelled doom for two years of our work, not to mention our future plans.

How can you avoid a scenario like the one we had on our hands? Once you have your project idea well defined, you've got to let everyone know about it. Communicating your goals, your ideas, and your progress is essential to successful product management. As they say, "out of sight, out of mind." Keep your project front and center.

Gut check with an elevator pitch

An elevator pitch is an informal tool. Before you put a lot of effort into presentation materials, you can get a quick gut pulse check on people's feelings about your project. Are they interested? Do they have pointers or suggestions for people they think you should talk to who may have been down the same path before? Is your idea in conflict with another roadmap you weren't aware of? Or even better, synergistic with it? The elevator pitch is a dirt cheap way to get quick feedback.

What makes a good elevator pitch?

The elevator pitch should explain to someone, ideally in a single pithy statement, what your project is all about. What makes a good elevator pitch? Your goal is to explain quickly and concisely three things: 1) what you're building, 2) for whom, and 3) why it matters. An elevator pitch absolutely must explain the value brought to actual people. Just fill in this template: We'll *"do this thing"* for *"some audience"* in order to *"achieve some important result"*.

The biggest mistake people make with an elevator pitch is to describe the thing being built, rather than the value it brings to users. The second is they don't explain why it matters.

For example, a bad elevator pitch is, "We're creating a glue that dries in 60 seconds." A better elevator pitch is, "We're creating a quick-drying glue that lets you repair anything around your house in under a minute." A bad elevator pitch is, "We're building a chat technology with built-in translation." A better elevator pitch is, "We're building a chat with built-in translation to help non-English speakers communicate with our customer support team."

But how do you make it even better? You need to supply a bit of data that explains why this is a problem that needs to be solved. For example, "The average user can save $500 per year by repairing broken items instead of replacing them, and our glue will only cost $5." Or, "Our studies show that 35% of our customers have problems communicating with customer support due to language barriers – this technology is expected to increase custom retention by 10%."

Your elevator pitch should answer the question, "So what?"

Formalize with a vision deck

Pitching is how you align stakeholders and decision makers that your vision, strategy or plan is the right one. In some sense, you should always be pitching – in the halls, at lunch, in elevators, etc. But in addition to warming people up in this way, you're also going to need to formally pitch people with a more structured message. A presentation (often called a vision deck) is the way you'll do this. A typical presentation will answer the following questions:

- What is the problem being solved?
- What is the opportunity, sometimes referred to as the *white space* where the solution can fit in and succeed?
- What is the proposed solution?

- Why is your plan the right one? Why do you think you will succeed?
- How will you measure success?
- What are the risks?
- Roughly how much time and money (or staff) will it take to get it done?

Go on a roadshow

You'll need the help of others to make your goals a reality. Nothing big is done solo – especially in a large organization. You need to get everyone on board early and keep them updated regularly to avoid eleventh hour surprises.

Because so many people can make or break your success, you want them to be bought into your project early. A roadshow is critical because it establishes familiarity with your project ahead of the time when decisions about your product need to be made. The earlier everyone knows about your work, the better your chance of positive outcomes. A roadshow let's others know what you're up to, and gives you an opportunity to let your audience know that their input is important to you.

Break your roadshow audience down into four groups: sponsors, partners, team members, and gatekeepers, and be sure to visit them all.

Sponsors

To get resources (people and money) allocated to your project, you may need an executive sponsor to vouch for your project's necessity within the company. Sometimes sponsors will be outside your immediate business unit. Does your project have benefits to other parts of your company – now or in the future? If so, getting leaders in other parts of the company interested and on board can be of great value to you. The more alignment you can build with leaders who believe your work is important, the likelier you are to succeed.

Cross-functional

Cross-functional partners lead disciplines needed to successfully launch a product. Marketing will have a say in how, where, and when your project gets communicated. And your legal team will help you understand risks, or may shut your project down if you haven't adequately thought through all the risks ahead of time. The list goes on.

Team members

These are the people who work on your projects directly – for example, engineers and UX designers in a tech company. Teams often have competing priorities so they need to be convinced this work is the most important.

Gatekeepers

These people control access to resources you need to succeed. Perhaps you're counting on a particular distribution channel, and it's tightly controlled. Or you need to schedule your launch with a release engineer amidst your company's other launches. All of these functional partners need to be aware that your project is coming down the pipe.

Set up meetings with all your stakeholders. In these meetings, your goals are the following:

- get across your vision and your high level plan
- solicit feedback from the stakeholder
- let them know exactly what kind of support you need

Your first road show should start very early in your process when you're looking for directional feedback. If you're going to get harsh feedback, you want it as early as possible so that you can course correct.

Pre-wiring

I was first introduced to the concept of pre-wiring in the book *The McKinsey Mind: Understanding and Implementing the Problem-Solving Tools and Management Techniques of the World's Top Strategic Consulting Firm*, by Ethan M. Rasiel and Paul N. Friga. There are many useful frameworks and tips in that book, and I highly recommend reading it.

If you're going to give a formal presentation to a group,

you should do a series of 1-on-1 presentations (also its own roadshow) with all of the key participants before the formal presentation. For example, let's say you will have a product review meeting where you hope to get executive buy-in for your product strategy. Try to get in front of everyone who will be part of the review meeting *before* it happens.

That may seem like an awful lot of work – it is – but it's worth it. By walking key people through your materials in advance, you get their feedback in a low-stakes environment. That gives you time to incorporate their ideas into your presentation before the real presentation. When they see their own DNA in your presentation because you got their feedback ahead of time, they're going to cheer lead your idea, because they're also now cheerleading their own idea. When decision makers see your presentation for the first time in a high-stakes meeting with senior leaders, they'll often point out flaws in order to prove how sharp they are.

Hearing your pitch more than once gives your audience familiarity with it. Having heard the pitch once makes them more receptive to it when they hear it a second time in the high-stakes meeting. This is called "pre-wiring". You're priming people to react in the best possible way to your presentation ahead of the high-stakes review.

In summary, don't get your ideas shut down simply because you haven't talked to stakeholders ahead of time. Get them familiar with your work and find any opportunity you can to build your stakeholders' good ideas and DNA into your vision, plans and pitches. You will instantly create your best cheerleaders by doing so.

> ### Recommended reading
>
> *The McKinsey Mind: Understanding and Implementing the Problem-Tools and Management Techniques of the World's Top Strategic Consulting Firm, by Ethan M. Rasiel and Paul N. Friga.*
>
> *This book contains many useful frameworks and ways of thinking, and I highly recommend reading it.*

Formal approvals

If you're lucky, your company may already have an approvals process for product launches. Often this approvals process is an afterthought, reviewed late in the game when you're ready to launch and looking for formal approvals. But you can use the approvals process at the very first stage of your project as a cheat-sheet to see whose buy-in you'll need down the road. Extract the list of the people, functions, and teams that will need to approve your work later, and get them on your side early.

If you're in a young company that doesn't already have an approvals process, you can start with the functions listed earlier in this book in the section, *Get to know your team*. Talk to each functional leader and ask them who else they think would be good to brief about your product launch. Find ways to document their buy-in. If this is the situation you're in, you can go above and beyond by documenting a repeatable approvals process as you work through it yourself. Socialize it within your organization. You'll make the task of getting buy-in easier for yourself next time, and every other product manager in the organization down the road.

But just the people listed in a formal approvals process aren't the only ones you need to brief and get buy-in from. The approvals list should be the bare minimum to launch – but you need the whole team bought in throughout the product life cycle to make headway. My SVP wasn't on any formal approvals list, but of course he had ultimate authority to kill a project.

To end the suspense regarding my team's feature nearly getting killed at the last moment, we *did* launch our changes to Android networking. It required a fast dash of roadshows to all of our SVP's key advisors, who he relied on to make his decisions. They were closer to our work and understood what we were doing. Once their support was secured, they were able to assure their boss the "bug" was nothing to worry about. And we were thus able to launch what was one of the biggest changes to Android's networking in memory.

Know the organization

Knowing who's who in your organization is really important. It's also important to actually *know* the people, not just know who they are. Some companies have excellent org charts that allow you to visualize how everyone is connected together. These are a great tool to start to see how the organization fits together.

But often a chart showing the management reporting chain won't give you the full picture. Often larger organizations are organized functionally. In that case, it will be hard to know who your cross-functional partners are by looking at an org chart because all the marketing folks will report to other marketing folks and may not be related in the chart to your team at all. Product managers are a good example of this phenomenon, also. Since product managers manage through influence, not reporting lines, how would anyone know what product managers are working on which products without asking? The same is true in reverse. The only way to learn who leads marketing for a given product area is to ask people.

In order to keep track of who you need to know, I suggest creating a spreadsheet where you track who's who in your organization. It will be especially helpful as a cheat-sheet for parts of the organization that you work with less frequently. I track people's name, email, title/function (legal, marketing, etc), who they report to, and any key notes to remember. I split my spreadsheet into sections for different teams.

Whenever you learn of someone who may become important to your work, set up time to meet with them. This should be an informal meeting just to get to know them and to learn about what they're working on and what their priorities are. It's best to get to know people informally well in advance of coming to them with a request to sponsor or approve your project.

Execution

Keeping focus is essential to not getting your product direction derailed. That goes equally well for your team as well as yourself. The next sections will discuss how to keep focus so your product direction doesn't drift, or worse.

Frame up working meetings

Product managers run a lot of meetings. In this section I'm going to teach you an intangible skill that will make your meetings more successful, thereby making your projects more successful.

People show up to meetings because the meeting is on their calendar. Often people are still thinking about their last meeting, or an email they want to send after your meeting is over. Often people show up to meetings and keep their laptops open so they can respond to pings on chat, or their phones are in their hands, scrolling throughout the meeting. They're working on something else while you're counting on them to help you move things forward. You need to remind people why they're in the room and what you need from them, or they're likely to not even know what's going on

I am not one to throw the first stone. I myself am guilty of having sat through entire meetings completely engrossed in what was happening on my laptop, paying no attention to what was happening in the room.

With this level of context switching and distraction present in our workdays, jumping right into problem solving without first setting context risks losing your meeting participants before the meeting has even begun. Repeating the narrative helps bring people back to the mission. A key habit to form is to start every working meeting with a quick reiteration of your narrative. This gives everyone in the meeting context about the state of your project, as well as a reminder of why they're in the meeting in the first place.

If you're skeptical, consider the opposite approach. Have you ever been in a meeting that jumped right into problem solving, leaving you or someone else lost? You weren't certain of exactly what was being discussed or what was the goal a subgroup of participants were fervently attacking? When there's no context, it's hard for everyone to participate. Most people are scared to ask dumb sounding questions like, "Wait, what is everyone talking about?" Given that uncertainty, of course it's easier to open up your laptop and look busy.

What is the best way to set context? I like to think of context in three pieces: the big picture, the current subgoal, and the now:

- First, what's the *big picture*? You can use your elevator pitch here.
- Next state your current objective: what critical part of the project the group in the room is driving toward, and by when do they need to hit the milestone?
- Finally, state the key change that needs to happen now to progress your project forward. What do you want to

accomplish in the meeting itself?

For example, "Hi all. We're working on the new time travel widget. Our goal is to build a prototype by the end of the year, and by the end of this month we want to lock in the user journeys. Today we're looking for approval on the UX mocks."

I remember this framework as "Big picture, Here, and Now."

Let's break that down:

- Big picture: We're building a time travel widget.
- Here: A prototype by the end of the year, and user journeys by the end of the month.
- Now: Approval of the UX mocks.

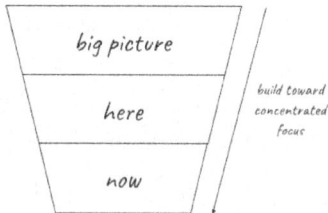

You can use a narrative like this one in every meeting you have. That includes meetings with your team, even though you have every reason to believe they *already know* the narrative. Here's why:

192

First, make sure you actually need the meeting. If there's no "now" aspect to your meeting, then you may be attending the meeting simply because it's on *your* calendar. If you don't know why you're having the meeting, cancel it. There's nothing more frustrating than arriving to a meeting to learn it has no agenda and then watching the minutes of your day evaporate.

Second, it's very easy to think that what's important to you is important to everyone else. That couldn't be further from the truth. Everyone has their own priorities and challenges to contend with. By constantly reminding others what the mission is, you help keep the project goals top of mind.

Third, the "Rule of 7" says that people need to hear something seven times before they'll remember it. You should expect that even your own team needs to hear the same message from you at least seven times before it has sunk in. When I hear this rule, I don't hear that I have to share my narrative exactly seven times. I hear that I have to share it *every* time.

It will feel awkward to repeat your narrative over and over again at first, and then it will become natural. In fact, continuous context-setting will help establish you as a leader. As the person who is consistently establishing context and direction, the team will start to look to you for that context and direction. You won't just be another person who shows up to the meeting; from the moment you set the context and the goals, you *are* leading.

Do you really have time for that at the start of every single meeting? Yes, you do. This intro can be quick and purposeful so you can get down to business.

Once you get the hang of it and see the impact this small but important practice can have, you'll wonder how you ever ran a meeting without it.

Another name for this is "beating the drum". You don't just hit the drum once and assume that was enough for everyone to stay on the same page forever. No. You need to keep the drum beat alive. You've got to keep beating the drum until the mission is accomplished.

Managing disagreement

If you've beat the drum about the product vision, at least everyone will know where you stand. But it doesn't mean everyone agrees.

It's the leader's job to help resolve differences of opinion and conflict about product direction. The first step to resolving conflict is spotting it. When you hear the term "conflict," you may think of loud angry dissent, but many people deliver their discontent quietly or passively. Unaddressed issues can lead to bigger problems down the road. A quiet team member may believe they're telegraphing their discontent to the leader through their silence. It's a leader's job to spot these potential problems when they're nascent.

When there is disagreement, it's the product manager's job to bring the team through a process that arrives at a resolution. How do you do that?

When there's disagreement, your first thought may be, "How do I convince this person of my opinion?" That is an instinct that needs to be kept in check. While making persuasive arguments is often useful as an individual contributor on the team, a leader needs to avoid "convincing" people at all costs. It turns out that nobody wants to be convinced of anything. Everybody wants to see that a decision aligns with their own needs and values. They want to come to a conclusion themselves.

To be a leader, not a dictator, you have to be open to being wrong, which you'll never discover if you spend all your time convincing others. And you certainly don't make a decision based on who wins a battle of wills, where there is a winner and a loser. It's 100% counterproductive to make your cross-functional team feel like they are losers. Your job is to extract the knowledge of your team to help make the best decision.

Second, don't make compromises that leave everyone half satisfied. Consensus is an ideal, but it is usually hard to achieve – even for an inconsequential decision like what toppings to put on a pizza. When we compromise in an attempt to give *everyone* a little of what they want, the solution often satisfies *no one* in particular. The infamous term "Design by committee" springs to mind.

Instead of these tactics, find agreement by working as a team to dissect a problem thoroughly until the right solution emerges. The remainder of this section discusses tactics to find agreement. I'll focus on finding truths that can bring everyone to the same conclusion – note that the conclusion might not be the original place where you started:

- Establish a gut check on whether the team is bought into the vision
- Make sure everyone has been heard and more importantly *feels* heard
- When the team doesn't agree on specifics, work to agree on principles

Sometimes disagreements can't be resolved. Or, you may be dealing with a larger force that can't be changed. In these circumstances, you still have options that allow you to move forward:

- Agree to disagree
- Practice Aikido by sidestepping the conflict and redirecting energy

Let's dive into these one by one.

Is everyone bought into the vision?

Often it's not so simple as asking people for more information, clarifying goals, and expecting everything to work itself out. Sometimes people don't agree that the product you want to build, or the direction you want to go, is the right direction.

Different people on your team may have perfectly valid ideas about what would make for a nice improvement from the status quo. There may be as many good ideas as there are people.

This may be a problem of matching your narrative with their needs and values. You may need to reframe. Are you asking the team to make too big of a leap of faith in one go? Can you break down the vision into a sequence where the first step seems less risky? It's possible that you see an elephant but your team sees elbows and ears. Your team is not to blame when this happens.

If your team doesn't agree on the vision, either they need more information, or they need to hear it framed in a different way. Figure out which it is and get everyone on the same page. Always approach disagreements humbly and accept that it may be you who is wrong. The worst outcome is a stalemate where either the project doesn't move forward, or team members decide to move on.

Return to the vision and adjust as needed to make sure the team can buy into it before you try to solve local disagreements about next steps. Debating next steps when there isn't broad agreement on the vision itself is like rearranging deck chairs on the titanic. You may feel great about brokering an agreement for what the team will do tomorrow, but your ship may still sink.

Feeling heard

People who have opposing or unpopular views need to feel heard. As a leader, you need to find safe ways to bring diverse viewpoints out into the open, so that misunderstandings or disagreements can be resolved.

An astute leader needs to pick up on small signals. For example, conflict may present itself as someone being uncharacteristically quiet in a meeting, not telling you what's really on their mind. It's up to the leader to notice these quiet team members and ask them what they think. He may have been silently fuming: "I'm just sitting here, and I know the most about this topic, and she doesn't even ask me what I think!" Bring him back into the fold by reaching out and asking. "Jim, you've been quiet today. What do you think about this proposal?" Jim, given the stage, may give you an earful. By hearing what's on Jim's mind, the team may either decide to investigate something new, or adjust course; or, someone may have some information that makes Jim feel okay with the current direction. You may learn a lot, and hopefully you can make a quiet, seething team member an ally rather than a non-believer.

You can also put Jim to work. Ask him to enumerate the pros and cons of his proposal versus the current plan of record. You might find some information that was overlooked. Or maybe using their list of pros and cons, you'll have a more straightforward way to address their concerns. You may not ultimately go with their proposal in its entirety, but at least you can ensure that they felt heard. Often that's just as important to employees as having their idea win.

Sometimes conflict is due to lack of information, or a simple misunderstanding of goals. In those cases, more clarity from product sponsors or more product definition is needed to iron out any areas of ambiguity that had allowed for multiple conflicting understandings to flourish.

Agree on principles

Your team may agree on the long term vision, and even agree on the next step. They've agreed on the *Why* and the *What*. But they may not agree with the *How*.

Often there are complex tradeoffs in big decisions. In products, ease of use may trade off with configurability and user control. Simplicity may trade off with transparency. Quality trades off with cost, and so on.

Don't let these elephants in the room go unspoken. Does everyone agree that the highest quality materials are going to be used in all instances, final bill of materials to be damned? Does everyone agree users shouldn't have to make decisions that you can make for them, or do some team members firmly believe the best product is one that's ultra configurable for power users? Questions like these are the realm of principles. Principles are overarching statements that help inform *how* you will build your product or carry out your big ideas.

Understanding who your intended users are and what their expectations are helps establish principles. Sometimes reminding the team that they and the user are not the same person and don't have the same needs helps to put things in perspective.

The team should agree on principles, and the prioritization of principles that are in tension with one another. With sufficient principles to set boundaries on the *How*, conflicts around the *How* should naturally disappear. When your existing principles don't resolve an open question, focus your efforts on deriving a new guiding principle rather than debating the specific problem at hand in isolation.

As much as we might like to establish all the principles up front, assuming that will make the rest of the product definition and development process a cake-walk, in practice it's usually very difficult to come up with principles before you've encountered some conflict or difference of opinion on the team. Conflict exposes an area where expectations or values aren't equal between two parties. Working out these differences is how you derive a new principle or value for the working team.

Exercise: What do you have to believe?

Often teams resort to enumerating pros and cons for multiple options. But these lists aren't helpful when there isn't a clear way to weigh the pros and cons against one another. For example, purchasing a more expensive component may have a strategic benefit by establishing a relationship with a partner you need as an ally; or the cheaper option may carry more execution risk.

An exercise I call "What do you have to believe?" can get you unstuck in these situations. Make a table with three columns. The first column is an identifier – always label options so they're easy to refer to as Option 1, Option 2, etc. The second column is a description of the option. The third column answers "What do you have to believe?"

The task for the team is to work out the third column, identifying what has to be true for the option to be the right one. Now the problem is no longer about convincing anyone that one option is better or worse than another via pros and cons. Now the work is about which reality is most likely to be true. Some options will get crossed out because "what you have to believe" for it to be the top option actually wasn't believable.

See below for an example exercise to determine the best marketing option. Note that this exercise works well in the workplace as well as for decision making in life.

> *Option 1: Direct response email marketing*
> *Have to believe: Our marketing will get beyond spam filters*

> *Option 2: Direct response mailers*
> *Have to believe: It can be done for less than $0.25 per piece*

> *Option 3: Broad-based brand advertising*
> *Have to believe: We can tie purchases back to the ads*

Sidestep conflict: Practice Aikido

Better than winning a conflict is not having a conflict at all. You can't lose a battle you never get into.

Typically when we think of martial arts, we think of a blur of kicks and punches thrown. Some are blocked and some land hard. Both opponents try to take the other out by landing hits to the body. The winner is the fastest or strongest.

Aikido is a Japanese martial art that looks very different from the others. Aikido relies on nonresistance in order to sidestep the partner's power. Aikido practitioners don't block punches, they step out of the way of them. They don't try to stop incoming forces, they redirect them a few degrees. Aikido is the art of using the opponent's force and energy to your own benefit, and getting out of the way when necessary. When you watch an Aikido match, you don't see the impact of two opposing forces – what you see is like a dance.

Look for ways to side-step conflict whenever possible. This does not mean compromise or ignoring the other party. It means getting out of the way of an oncoming train rather than trying to stop it. Remember that we're not meant to be "opponents" in the workplace. Don't get crushed in intractable battles. Instead, let the train go by. Understand where it's going. Hop on it if possible and ride it. It's always easier to attach yourself to existing momentum than to try to stop it head on.

If all else fails, agree to disagree

Sometimes resolving a conflict comes down to a judgment call. Someone has to make a decision. Depending on the organization, the final call may be made by the product manager, or escalated to higher ups. Once the decision is made, hopefully everyone can move on and implement the decision. This is called "disagree and commit".

For "disagree and commit" to work, everyone has to feel that they were heard, even if their position was not the one that ultimately won out. Ideally those who disagreed can at least see some of their DNA in the final solution.

Disagree and commit should always be the last resort. It's good to have this escape hatch, and it's important to know when to stop trying to get everyone on the same page and optimize instead for making a decision quickly. But people who didn't get their way may still feel bruised. If they're asked to disagree and commit repeatedly, they'll feel their opinions aren't valued, and they may be less likely to offer up opinions in your next project. Ultimately, they may leave your team to go work somewhere that they feel more valued. So don't rely on this approach too much.

Recommended reading

Multipliers, by Liz Wiseman, is an amazing book to help you learn how to get the most out of a team.

The book outlines the habits of leaders that drive teams to work harder than they ever thought possible through setting appropriate goals and challenges, and perhaps most importantly, by *not* trying to force your will on others.

While this book is primarily aimed at people managers, all of the concepts are equally valid for Product Managers. If there is a book I wish I had read earlier in my career, this is it.

Managing yourself

"If you want something done, ask a busy person.
—Benjamin Franklin

If you are a "doer" like me, it's likely that you're simultaneously engulfed in a lot of projects – both personally and professionally. That's typical for product managers. Juggling a dozen projects at once and somehow making it all work is certainly impressive. But it's rare to be able to keep that up forever. Most likely that kind of work can lead to burnout.

With so much multitasking, it's unlikely that any project will get the full attention it deserves. You may have a lot of projects that get done half as well, or worse – that only get half done. The saying "Less is more" is true. When you focus on fewer simultaneous projects, you can put more of your and your team's resources into doing the job completely and with high quality. You can put "more wood behind fewer arrows."

There are some evenings where I can barely remember what happened that day. It's because so many different things happened, and yet very little progress was made toward goals. Whenever it feels like there are too many concurrent "top priorities", I need to reestablish focus.

But even when you've got your own focus, there's a limit to how much you can do on your own.

There are only two ways to get more done in this world. The first is to focus, paradoxically, on fewer things. The second is to find ways to scale beyond yourself.

There are three tactics that I use to reestablish focus when my list of concurrent projects becomes eye-popping and I feel like I'm not making any real progress: I establish my One Thing, write a shortlist, eliminate or offload, and establish a daily focus.

What's your One Thing?

An excellent book by Gary Keller, *The One Thing*, helps clarify why it's so important to have a narrow focus to be successful. Narrow focus doesn't mean you don't get a lot done – just the opposite. It means you have a lot of impact within a focused band. Here are some examples from Gary's domain, real estate.

As a real estate agent, should you focus on being buyers' agent *and* a sellers' agent? What about leasing rentals, too? The three require very different skills. If you spread yourself across all of them, how good can you get at any of them in particular?

One approach to working is to be opportunistic and make the most out of any opportunity that comes your way. But when you try and do it all, you can get spread too thin. When the types of work you take on are too dissimilar, you don't get any benefits from repeatability. Expertise you gained in one area – including any process or infrastructure you've set up – may be of no use in other areas.

Another approach is to be more selective. Plot out your goals and work tirelessly toward them. In this approach, you'll see random "opportunities" as distractions and you'll be less likely to jump on them. Instead, you'll eliminate them before they prevent you from achieving your true goals.

Maintain a Shortlist

Every couple months, I revisit a list of the projects I'm devoting my time to. Each time I revisit the list, I add any new projects I've gotten myself involved in, and I remove anything that I've completed.

I feel lighter when I get to remove something, and I often feel a bit of sadness when I add something when deep down I know there's really no room for it. I think, why did I volunteer myself for a new project? Didn't I realize that it was going to consume more of my time than I have available?

The next step is to put the list in priority order, with the most important items at the top. No two items can be of equal importance. When everything is considered a top priority, then nothing is really the top priority.

Once the list is in order, I draw a line to establish my shortlist. Above the line are the projects I will continue to devote effort to. Everything below the line needs to be paused or fully divested. This may mean formally resigning from actual commitments. That sounds drastic and at first I felt this was an act of abandonment – that those I was pulling away from would be devastated when I told them I didn't have time for their project any longer. In fact, when you don't have time for something, the people you're working with are usually happy to be free to choose a replacement who can devote more attention than you can, without having to formally kick you out.

Keep the list above the line very short. At work, more than five projects just doesn't feel realistic. Below the line are projects that may still be important, but need to temporarily go on pause or be given away in order for you to put "more wood behind fewer arrows." Only by focusing my energies on completing a discrete number of projects do I truly have a shot at crossing them off the list.

Find leverage points

One of Gary Keller's insights is *The One Thing* is to identify something you can do that makes the rest of your task list either easier or completely unnecessary.

That may be adding technology to replace repetitive tasks. For example, if you're answering support emails one by one, would canned responses, or even a bot help eliminate this work?

If many of the bugs in your product are coming from a very complex feature and it's not the most important feature anyway, can you free up time and resources by eliminating the feature rather than trying to fix it?

If you have a tendency to try to do every aspect of a project yourself, think through who might be better to partner with early on. For example, can you loop in a project manager to work out the schedule with the engineering team right from the start? Even if there isn't much work for a project manager at first, if you bring them on early, they'll have more context when the project is in full swing.

Similarly, can you bring in a data scientist right from the start to think through how what you're doing may impact other parts of the product? While you might be able to think through some of the data-driven investigations yourself, you only have so much headspace, and a data scientist is likely to have better tools at their disposal than you do, anyway.

So it goes with all aspects of a project when you're a product manager. Can you find people who are experts who you can leverage? While you may be a good stop gap, experts can do more in their areas of expertise than you can yourself, leading to better results than when you try to go it alone.

Freeing up your time outside of work is important, too. Let's face it, being a product manager is a demanding job. You'll appreciate having more time to relax when you're not working. I often get in my head that I'll undertake home improvement projects on my own, such as repainting my house or doing gardening. But once those things become "projects" that I'm squeezing into my already packed schedule, then I need to rethink whether I'm the best person for the job. Many people can paint walls, but only I can write my book. Hire someone to do mundane tasks that take your time, but which don't require your expertise to get the job done.

Establish a daily focus

Establishing a daily focus is critical. We've all experienced days where we are driven by our Inbox. When we respond to every incoming message, all these people sending us messages suddenly become our bosses.

A daily focus is a form of "all wood, *one* arrow" practiced day by day.

I manage my own daily focus through a simple document that has three sections. The first is my focus mantras. The second is my shortlist. The third contains my daily goals. Once you create this document, schedule 15 minutes each morning to review it and adjust.

Here's what's at the top of my focus document, my matras:

What's the most important thing I can do today?
Do it and go home.

DON'T READ EMAIL.
CANCEL UNNECESSARY MEETINGS.

THINK BIG.
THINK SCALE.
PRIORITIZE LEVERAGED ACTIVITIES.

Beneath this header of mantras, I write my shortlist of my current focus areas – a maximum of five projects.

Beneath that list, every Monday, I manually write out the dates for the work week. Beside each date, I write one thing and one thing only that would be a key accomplishment for that day. I don't just write the name of the project that I'm going to work on. An "accomplishment" is a deliverable that will move the project forward.

For example:

```
Mo: Complete all peer reviews
Tu: Draft pitch deck for project X
We: Schedule all road shows with stakeholders within
the next 2 weeks for project Y
Th: Resolve prioritization issues team is having in
project Z
Fr: Complete bi-weekly bug triage project
```

In addition to reviewing my daily goals, each day I have to make sure I actually have time to accomplish my goal for the day, which means eliminating distractions. As it says in the header, "DON'T READ EMAIL" and "CANCEL UNNECESSARY MEETINGS". Until you've achieved your goal, push off anything less important that sucks up your time.

It may seem crazy to only have one goal for each day. Just remember that many people, at the end of a week, cannot identify what was moved forward during that entire week, let alone a given day. They answered a lot of email, they attended a lot of meetings. They may have done some incremental work here and there. Yet they may have few or no accomplishments that actually moved their projects forward or got them closer to crossing those projects off their list altogether. If you accomplish just one nameable achievement each day – *that's five achievements per work week, twenty per month, 240 per year!* – you're going to be miles ahead of everyone else.

Finally, take note that there are only five days in the work week. If you plan to achieve one big thing per day, then this means if you have more than five projects in flight at once, it's unlikely you're going to make progress on each one on a weekly basis. That's why it's so important to have a *short* shortlist – keep it at five projects or fewer.

In conclusion

Now you've got it all: You learned about the team. You learned how to develop a vision and strategy. You've seen the steps of the product development life cycle and you know how to validate an idea at each stage. You know the tools of the trade that get the job done, and you've dipped your toe into process development. You have an understanding of how to socialize your message in the organization and build consensus for product ideas. Most importantly, you know how to focus the team and how to focus yourself. Now it's up to you to put this knowledge to good use. I wish you good luck in all your endeavors and all your products.

I hope you enjoyed this book. Please help others by posting your review on Amazon.

Printed in Great Britain
by Amazon